Published under the auspices of
The Center for Japanese Studies
University of California, Berkeley

Peasant Protests and Uprisings in Tokugawa Japan

STEPHEN VLASTOS

Peasant Protests and Uprisings in Tokugawa Japan

UNIVERSITY OF
CALIFORNIA PRESS
Berkeley   Los Angeles   London

University of California Press
Berkeley and Los Angeles, California
University of California Press, Ltd.
London, England
© 1986 by
The Regents of the University of California
Printed in the United States of America
1 2 3 4 5 6 7 8 9

Chapter 7 appeared, in slightly different form,
as "Yonaoshi in Aizu" in T. Najita and J. V.
Koschmann, eds., *Conflict in Modern Japanese
History: The Neglected Tradition,* and is reprinted
with permission.© by Princeton University
Press.

Library of Congress Cataloging in Publication Data

Vlastos, Stephen, 1943–
    Peasant protests and uprisings in Tokugawa Japan.

    Bibliography: p.
    Includes index.
    1. Peasant uprisings–Japan.   2. Japan–Social
conditions– 1600-1868.   3. Fukushima-ken (Japan)–
Social conditions.   I. Title.
DS871.5.V56   1986   952'.025   85-5832
ISBN 0-520-04614-5

For Mary Ann

Contents

Maps

Tables

Acknowledgments

Many individuals and institutions in the United States and Japan gave me invaluable assistance during the writing of this book. As a graduate student at the University of California, Berkeley, I had the good fortune to work with Irwin Scheiner, whose intellect and warmth helped to make those years a rewarding period, and with Thomas C. Smith, whose outstanding work in Tokugawa social and economic history initially inspired, and continue to influence, my own research. Paul Greenough, David Arkush, and Alan Spitzer, colleagues at the University of Iowa, read my manuscript and gave me useful criticisms, as did Richard Smethurst, Anne Walthall, Theda Skocpol, and Temma Kaplan. I also thank the editors at the University of California Press, Berkeley, for their patience and Jesse Phillips for his careful manuscript editing.

The debt I owe to scholars and friends in Japan is even greater. Irokawa Daikichi helped me at every turn. I could not have written this book without drawing on the voluminous research of Shōji Kichinosuke, who made time in his busy schedule on numerous occasions to advise me. Hashimoto Mitsuru was a good friend and stern critic; Kobayashi Seiji, Honda Hiroshi, Mori Tateshi, Ōishi Kaichirō, and Ei Hideo helped me in many ways for which I shall always be grateful.

Finally, I received generous financial support from the Social Science Research Council, the American Council of Learned Societies, the National Endowment for the Humanities, the Center for Japanese Studies at the University of California, Berkeley, the Japan Foundation, and the University of Iowa.

1. Introduction

Conflict and Collective Action

My analysis of peasant movements in Japan of the Tokugawa period (1600–1867) proceeds from the generally Marxist assumption, which is shared by some non-Marxists, that disruptive actions by socially subordinate groups such as peasants are important, but not abnormal, events in states where property, power, rights, and privileges are distributed unequally among the principal social classes.[1] This is not to claim that social conflict necessarily finds expression in collective action organized around classes—still less that oppressed people will act in terms of objective class interests. Instead, the assumption leads me to adopt a particular analytic strategy. The movements represented collective efforts by peasants to resist the authority of the warrior ruling class as it impinged on their daily lives, and as such reveal the structure and character of class relations in the Tokugawa polity. By analyzing the form and content of rural conflict and changes from the early to the late Tokugawa period, we can discover how particular political and economic structures affected peasants' capacity to act in pursuit of their interests.

1. Rudolfo Stavenhaven, *Social Classes in Agrarian Societies* (Garden City, N.Y., 1975), pp. 26–27.

The conception of conflict as an integral and dynamic force in societal development is largely absent from most of the scholarship devoted to popular movements which has been produced in the United States and Great Britain since the Second World War. Whether drawing on the theoretical work of Durkheim or Parsons, social scientists who use consensus and structural-functional models of social systems conceive of conflict as pathological and interpret collective violence as evidence of the breakdown of the beliefs and institutions that integrate society.[2] Explicitly or implicitly the metaphor used is that of disease, which generates an imagery replete with infections, eruptions, and contagions.[3] Moreover, as doctor to the body politic, social scientists lavish attention on social movements in direct proportion to their perceived size and virulence. The problem is not simply that there are a hundred theoretical studies of revolutionary movements for every one which examines collective actions that aspire to less grandiose goals. After all, revolutions, and especially social revolutions, are unique and momentous events that brought about lasting changes in the politics, social structure, and economic relations of the revolutionary society and influenced the course of world history. I do not begrudge the fact that so much has been written about such a small number of historical events. My objection, rather, is to the almost universal tendency to attribute undue significance to violent expressions of social conflict, and to assume that they constitute a uniquely meaningful set of social phenomena. As Charles Tilly has pointed out, in most cases the occurrence of violence in conjunction with collective action has been brought on by the "heavy involvement of agents of the state, especially repressive agents like police and soldiers."[4] If the purpose is to understand the relationship between social

2. Chalmers Johnson, *Revolution and the Social System* (Stanford, Calif., 1964), pp. 3–10.

3. Edwin Black, "The Second Persona," *Quarterly Journal of Speech* 56 (April 1970): 109–119.

4. Charles Tilly, *From Mobilization to Revolution* (Reading, Mass., 1978), p. 177.

conflict and collective action, rather than the attitudes and behavior of the ruling class and its agents, it makes more sense to
treat both violent and nonviolent actions as belonging to the
same class of social phenomena. Returning to Tilly's important
insight: "Most collective violence . . . grows out of actions which
are not intrinsically violent, and which are basically similar to a
much larger number of collective actions occurring without violence in the same periods and settings."[5]

The point I wish to make is that violent collective actions tell
us something about the organized expression of social conflict,
but not everything we need to know. Where there are data on
nonviolent collective actions, they should be used, together
with the data on violent actions, to explore fully the structural
aspects of social conflict. This is particularly pertinent in the
case of Tokugawa peasant movements, since the majority involved little obvious disorder or destruction of state property.
Fatalities were even rarer, except for the harsh sentences meted
out by the state to punish the leaders and discourage repetition.
Anyone accustomed to using body counts as the measure of
significant conflict might well assume that there was little real
conflict between lord and peasant, and that the protests were
not terribly important. Nevertheless, owing to structural aspects of the lord-peasant relationship (discussed below), protests characterized by low levels of violence proved to be re-
markably effective in realizing peasants' collective interests.
Paradoxically, the largest and most violent collective actions by
peasants—the *yonaoshi*, or "world rectification," uprisings at the
end of the Tokugawa period—did not signify a higher level of
conflict between peasants and the ruling class, but chiefly conflict among peasants.[6]

To pursue the medical analogy further, there is what might
be called an etiological bias in much of the literature on popular movements. Because of the tendency to view disruptive

5. Ibid.
6. See chap. 6, below, the section "Mobilization in the Late Tokugawa
Period."

actions by subordinate classes as symptoms of disease, many scholars conceive of causes in terms of exogenous forces that produce stresses and strains in an otherwise healthy society, rather than as an integral aspect of social relations. By reducing causes to a set of independent variables, they offer explanations based on statistical correlations alone, and are likely to ignore the structural relations that made collective action possible in the first place. In a seminal essay which analyzed crowd actions in eighteenth-century England, E. P. Thompson pinpointed the most serious failings of this approach by noting that W. W. Rostow's "social tension chart" and other stimulus-response models "may conclude investigation at the exact point at which it becomes of serious sociological or cultural interest: being hungry (or being sexy), what do people do? How is their behavior modified by custom, culture, and reason?"[7]

It is not my purpose to attempt a systematic critique of theories of collective action based on consensus and structural-functional models of social systems. Tilly and other scholars have already done the job; and, in any case, the few Western-language studies of Tokugawa peasant movements happily do not fit the mold.[8] Rather, the point that I wish to emphasize is that how one views social conflict will largely determine what questions one will want to ask. Since I begin by assuming that

7. E. P. Thompson, "The Moral Economy of the English Crowd in the Eighteenth Century," *Past and Present* 50 (February 1971): 77–78.

8. Hugh Borton, *Peasant Uprisings in Japan of the Tokugawa Period* (1940; reprint., New York, 1968); W. Donald Burton, "Peasant Movements in Early Tokugawa Japan," *Journal of Peasant Studies* 8, no. 3 (1979): 162–181; Mitsuru Hashimoto, "The Social Background of Peasant Uprisings in Tokugawa Japan," in *Conflict in Modern Japanese History*, ed. Tetsuo Najita and J. V. Koschmann (Princeton, N.J., 1982), pp. 145–163; Irwin Scheiner, "Benevolent Lords and Honorable Peasants," in *Japanese Thought in the Tokugawa Period, 1600–1868*, ed. Tetsuo Najita and Irwin Scheiner (Chicago, 1978), pp. 39–62; Patricia Sipple, "Popular Protest in Early Modern Japan," *Harvard Journal of Asian Studies* 37 (December 1978): 273–322; and Anne Walthall, "Times of Protest: Commoners and Collective Action in Late Eighteenth Century Japan" (Ph.D. diss., University of Chicago, 1978). The one quantitative study in English is Yoshio Sugimoto, "Structural Sources of Popular Revolts and the *Tobaku* Movement at the Time of the Meiji Restoration," *Journal of Asian Studies* 34 (1975): 875–889.

conflict between lord and peasant was a central and continuing aspect of social relations, I am less interested in what set of conditions "caused" peasants to protest than in the nature, form, and content of the movements. The structure of conflict and what it can tell us about class relations is the primary concern; events that acted as triggers are secondary. The question most frequently asked is not why they disputed the terms of feudal rule, but how they did so, with what intent, to what effect.

Tokugawa Political Economy

Tokugawa feudalism differed in important respects both from earlier feudal orders in Japan and from those of medieval Europe. Although familiar to the Japanese specialist, the following overview will prepare the ground for the analysis of structural factors that affected collective action by peasants in the Tokugawa period.

The Tokugawa polity was characterized by a degree of political stability unparalleled among feudal societies.[9] From the early seventeenth century to the mid-nineteenth century, the shogun and his council of vassal daimyo, the Bakufu, exercised absolute and undisputed authority in the political realm. In part, stability was achieved by balancing central (shogun-Bakufu) and regional (daimyo) power within a polity characterized by rigid parcelization of sovereignty. After defeating a coalition of rival warlords at the battle of Sekigahara in 1600, Tokugawa Ieyasu claimed roughly a quarter of the country,

9. The reader is referred to the following studies of Tokugawa political and economic institutions: Harold Bolitho, *Treasures among Men* (New Haven, Conn., 1974); John W. Hall, *Government and Local Power in Japan, 500–1700* (Princeton, N.J., 1966), pp. 330–374; *Studies in the Institutional History of Early Modern Japan*, ed. John W. Hall and Marius Jansen (Princeton, N.J., 1968); Susan B. Hanley and Kozo Yamamura, *Economic and Demographic Change in Preindustrial Japan, 1600–1868* (Princeton, 1978); George Sansom, *History of Japan 1615–1867* (Stanford, Calif., 1963); Thomas C. Smith, *Agrarian Origins of Modern Japan* (Stanford, 1959); Conrad D. Totman, *Politics in the Tokugawa Bakufu, 1600–1843* (Cambridge, Mass., 1967).

including Edo, Osaka, and Kyoto, the three largest cities, as Tokugawa house land. The remainder was divided into fiefs (*han*)
and assigned to more than two hundred and fifty daimyo: "hereditary vassals" (*fudai* daimyo) and "outside lords" (*tozama* daimyo). The *fudai* daimyo had sworn fealty before the battle of
Sekigahara, and the most trusted among them sat on the Bakufu, which advised the shogun on policy, administered the Tokugawa territories, and attended to all other matters related to
the day-to-day running of the shogunate. The *tozama* daimyo,
who had sworn allegiance after Sekigahara, were assumed to be
less trustworthy and were excluded from the Bakufu. But
whether *fudai* or *tozama*, the considerable autonomy of daimyo
posed a threat to the political order, for although their status as
vassals was highly conditional, they were sovereign within their
fiefs. Daimyo maintained their own military organizations and
enjoyed full rights of exploitation over the commoner population, assessing taxes, commanding labor, and regulating trade,
in addition to enforcing law and order. They possessed considerable powers which were beyond the direct control of the shogun and the Bakufu; and since in the past simple oaths of fealty
had failed miserably in guaranteeing the obedience of vassals,
it was not long before the Tokugawa shogun established institutions designed to keep daimyo on a short leash. In 1635 Tokugawa Iemitsu, Ieyasu's talented grandson, instituted an elabo-
rate hostage system, the *sankin kōtai*, which required daimyo to
spend alternate years in residence at Edo, the shogun's castle
town, attending court. They were also required to maintain
stately houses in Edo for the heir apparent and first consort,
who lived permanently in the capital, attended by a sizable con-
tingent of samurai retainers and a large household staff.

   Sankin kōtai acted as an effective counterbalance to the political autonomy daimyo enjoyed as provincial feudal lords. Up to
half of their time and revenue was consumed in the purely ceremonial functions of attending the shogun's court and traveling
in stately procession between Edo and their fiefs, at which time
their activities were subject to close supervision by Bakufu officials. The expenses incurred by daimyo, however, and the

growth of Edo as a center of seigneurial consumption, accelerated the rise of a money economy and national markets, forces which ultimately undermined the feudal order. In order to pay the costs associated with *sankin kōtai,* daimyo annually sold large quantities of rice collected as taxes to merchants in Osaka, which quickly became the distribution and manufacturing center of a national monetized economy geared to the consumption needs of Edo's enormous warrior population. The immediate consequence was the growth of a wealthy merchant class and the indebtedness of daimyo and their retainers, whose consumption needs outpaced income earned from the sale of tax rice by the end of the seventeenth century. In the eighteenth century the growth of Edo and Osaka as major urban centers with populations of 1,000,000 and 350,000 respectively began to affect villages strategically positioned to supply cash crops such as cotton, silk, paper, sake, vegetable oil, lacquer, wax, charcoal, and handicrafts to these cities. In most regions the majority of the peasantry continued to subsist as traditional agriculturalists whose survival depended on the bounty of the harvest and how much feudal lords demanded as taxes. Nevertheless, commodity production and trade added a new dimension to village economic life. Investment in cash crops and agricultural by-employments provided much needed income which was also lightly taxed. At the same time, production for the market increased risks, and benefits were not distributed equally. Households which had the resources to profit from commodity production and trade acquired considerable wealth, often at the expense of small cultivators, some of whom were forced out of farming altogether. This weakened the feudal tax base and increased stratification and social tension within villages. By the late Tokugawa period, moneylending and landlord-tenant relationships were commonplace, as was production for the market even among the poorest peasant farmers. Thus, the juridically determined social order in which peasants were subsistence agriculturalists, as indeed they were in the early Tokugawa period, bore little relation to functional relationships within the market economy of late Tokugawa—circumstances which profoundly affected conflict and collective action at the end of Tokugawa rule.

The second distinctive feature of the Tokugawa polity was national isolation (*sakoku*). Even prior to 1600 fears of foreign intervention had led to restrictions on Christian missions.[10] After assuming power Tokugawa Ieyasu tightened controls on foreign intercourse by further restricting the activities of missionaries and by limiting overseas trade to his port cities, thereby depriving daimyo and merchants of the many benefits of direct links to the world economy. The final and radical severing of relations with the outside world, however, followed a militant peasant rebellion, the Shimabara rising of 1637/38, a revolt of religiously and economically oppressed peasants in southwestern Japan led by a messianic Christian convert.[11] Although not instigated or even abetted by foreigners, the rebellion showed all too clearly the dangerous influence of foreign ideas. In 1639 the Bakufu ended diplomatic relations with all countries except Korea and China, and forbade citizens to travel abroad. The only trade permitted was transacted at Nagasaki by licensed Chinese and Dutch trading companies under the most rigorous supervision. For the next two hundred years Japan's isolation was complete. Whatever the stresses and strains caused by the growth of the domestic market, the Tokugawa regency was not threatened by the importation of ideologies and technologies antithetical to the feudal order. And until the late 1850s, when Japan was forced to open its ports to foreign trade, the population was spared the disruptive impact of world markets on the domestic economy.

A third feature, and the most important for understanding the political economy of Tokugawa feudalism, was the absolute separation of the samurai and peasant classes, enforced in both Bakufu territory and private fiefs.[12] The reasons for the adop-

10. C. R. Boxer, *The Christian Century in Japan, 1549–1650* (Berkeley and Los Angeles, 1974), pp. 362–374.

11. Ivan Morris, *The Nobility of Failure* (New York, 1975), pp. 143–179; Fukaya Katsumi, *Hyakushō ikki no rekishiteki kōzō* (Tokyo, 1979), pp. 130–179.

12. Satsuma *han* was an exception; see Robert Sakai, *Status and Social Organization of Satsuma* (Tokyo, 1975), pp. 14–19.

tion of this policy are discussed in the next chapter, but here we note the implications for social relations. All samurai retainers were required to live in castle towns, where they subsisted on stipends drawn from the lord's storehouse. This arrangement eliminated subinfeudation and the last vestiges of the manorial (*shōen*) economy of the medieval (*chūsei*) period, and gave rise to new bureaucratic procedures of exploitation. Unable to command peasants' labor directly in agricultural production, the Tokugawa seigneurial class derived its revenue from land rents assessed on villages. Using detailed cadastral surveys of each village's farmland, whose productivity was measured in *koku* (5.1 bushels) of rice, officials calculated how much the peasants should pay and assigned yearly tax quotas, which the village headman was responsible for delivering to district collection offices. Villages were also assessed corvée labor for public works, and in some fiefs daimyo established monopolies on special agricultural products and manufacturing. But in most essential respects the relationship of lord to peasant producers was that of an absentee landlord—a claimant of the fruits of peasants' labor who did not supervise or manage agricultural production itself.

The removal of samurai to castle towns did not diminish the domination of daimyo over the peasantry. Even before 1600, warlords anxious to limit peasants' capacity to resist had systematically removed swords, spears, and other weapons from villages. The Tokugawa shogun continued the policy with characteristic efficiency, and by the middle of the seventeenth century the rural population had been effectively disarmed. Thereafter, the samurai monopoly on instruments of violence was very nearly complete, and legally samurai enjoyed the right to cut down on the spot any commoner who did not show proper deference—a provision of the legal code of greater symbolic than practical consequence, since neither shogun nor daimyo permitted wanton violence, but one which advertised that right, lest peasants forget that they were subordinate and defenseless.

Despite the undisputed power of the ruling class, the rigid spatial stratification of social classes created areas where peasants enjoyed considerable autonomy. Local administration was entrusted to peasant officials, and in most respects villages managed their political affairs free from direct supervision. A similar discontinuity existed in the economic sphere. Even though the Tokugawa system of land rents based on cadastral surveys initially proved to be an efficient mechanism of tax extraction, the seigneurial class did not directly manage the landed economy. Individually and communally peasants controlled the factors of agricultural production, which limited the actual power of daimyo as claimants, even in the seventeenth century when subsistence farming predominated. Later, after the development of markets and commodity production, the daimyo found it increasingly difficult to tax at the old rates.

Organization and Mobilization

One of the salient facts about peasants' movements in the Tokugawa period is that there were a great many of them. The exact number is not known, since in many cases the relevant primary sources—fief and village archives—were destroyed or lost long before historians realized their importance. Despite assiduous efforts made recently to mine collected materials and search out remaining caches of Tokugawa village documents, it is likely that some of the smaller movements, particularly nonviolent ones, have escaped detection. Nevertheless, the most complete record, Aoki Kōji's 1971 chronology, *Hyakushō ikki no sōgō nenpyō*, lists some three thousand peasant uprisings (*hyakushō ikki*) against seigneurial authority and another three thousand conflicts classified as intravillage disputes (*murakato sōdō*).[13] The Aoki data are far from complete; yet they show, on the average, more than twenty protests *and* disputes per year. As might be expected, peasants protested most frequently dur-

13. Aoki Kōji, *Hyakushō ikki sōgō nenpyō* (Tokyo, 1971). Aoki and most Japanese historians distinguish between antifeudal "peasant movements" (*hyakushō ikki*) and "struggles among villagers" (*murakata sōdō*). In the first, the peasants made demands to the seigneurial class, but in the second they did not directly dispute daimyo or Bakufu laws.

ing periods of famine and at the end of the era, when the Tokugawa hegemony collapsed. Peasants did not, however, limit protests to years of political turmoil and crop failure. The
minimum number of protests recorded in any one decade was
thirty, and the average was 113. Peasant protests were not
confined to any particular region or domain. Although there
were more in some regions than in others, they occurred in
every province and nearly every fief.[14]

Peasant protest was ubiquitous. The large number of protests, however, should not be interpreted as a measure of exploitation or discontent per se. Peasants, as Theda Skocpol has
pointed out, "always have justifiable grounds for rebellion,"[15]
but it is naïve to assume, as some political theorists do, that
discontent naturally finds expression in the form of opposition
movements or collective violence. Henry Landsberger, for example, reminds us that there are many societies in which "in-
tense peasant discontent has only rarely resulted in organized
protest, whether successful or not."[16] The first question to ask
with respect to the political behavior of Tokugawa peasants is
how to explain their demonstrated capacity to act collectively.
Here structural relationships were paramount.

The internal organization of the peasant class and its position within the Tokugawa polity were highly conducive to collective action. First, peasants formed a class, in the Marxist
sense, by virtue of occupying a common position with respect
to the means of production. At least until the latter half of the
eighteenth century, nearly all peasants were small-scale subsistence farmers who cultivated family-size holdings, using household labor. Although there were large and small homesteads,
the labor-intensive character of rice cultivation imposed an essential similarity on the style, uses, and organization of each
family's work force. Villagers also shared communal tasks, such
as maintaining and operating water-control systems, and

14. Ibid., app., p. 36.
15. Theda Skocpol, *States and Social Revolutions* (Cambridge, 1979), p. 115.
16. Henry Landsberger, "Peasant Unrest," in *Rural Protest*, ed. Landsberger
(London, 1974), pp. 1–2.

worked cooperatively during the periods of peak labor demand in the spring and autumn. Since even large landholders marketed only a small portion of the surplus product (the greater part being appropriated directly by the lord), there was little differentiation in economic roles. Families whose holdings exceeded their labor power absorbed collateral relatives and non-kin into the household labor force by using the ritual and terminology of extended kinships. Exploitation of peasants by other peasants, therefore, was masked, and possibly moderated, by norms of familial relationships, even when no blood relationship existed.[17] In the absence of landlord-tenant, credit-debtor, and employer–wage-laborer relations, the outward appearance and inner texture of community relations promoted solidarity within the village.

The structural relationship of lord to peasant also promoted peasants' awareness of their class interests. During the Tokugawa period, the seigneurial class appropriated surplus labor-value by means of a system of land rents assessed on the village in proportion to the size and assumed productivity of arable land. In principle, the tax absorbed the entire surplus, which left the cultivator only what was needed to satisfy subsistence needs; and indeed it is likely that the rate of tax extraction was initially very high. The relationship between peasant protests and the confiscatory nature of the land tax is a complex one to which we shall return. For the moment, however, the pertinent issue is the lord-peasant relation in its formal aspects rather than the degree of exploitation actually achieved. Following Arthur Stinchcombe, we note that several features of the relationship were likely to foster conflict consciousness.[18] First, the seigneurial class appropriated the surplus in the form of rents, assessed annually and collected in produce and cash. The process of exploitation was open and the value of what was appropriated easily measured. The issue of conflict was clear: what the lord took, the peasant lost. Second, to use the terminology

17. Smith, *Agrarian Origins*, p. 27.
18. Arthur Stinchcombe, "Agricultural Enterprises and Rural Class Relationships," *American Journal of Sociology* 62 (September 1962): 164–176.

of anthropologists, the economic relationship was single stranded;[19] peasants were not encumbered materially or psychologically by patron-client relationships with members of the ruling class. As we have seen, the Tokugawa seigneurial class exploited the landed economy as absentee landlords; living in distant castle towns, they did not actively organize, manage, or supervise agricultural production. Peasants generally possessed all the essential resources needed in small-scale farming, yet they were obliged to surrender a large portion of the harvest. The relationship was impersonal and remote, in addition to being conspicuously one-sided. Neither affective bonds born out of paternalistic relationships, nor dependency due to incomplete control of the means of production, obscured the exploitative relationship between the classes.

Structural relations which were conducive to achieving consciousness of interests also facilitated mobilization in their defense. Under Tokugawa law, the administrative village (*mura*) rather than the individual proprietor was the official unit of taxation. Within the village, paying taxes was an individual responsibility, but the village was corporately liable for the delivery of the cash and bales of rice that constituted final payment. Especially in the early Tokugawa period the collective obligations imposed by the tax system gave all peasants a strong material interest in resisting fiscal policies that threatened to drive marginal farm families into bankruptcy. Since the administrative village possessed a clearly delineated political structure, it served as the organizational basis of local mobilization—if, that is, a consensus existed as to appropriate forms of action. And, as residents of castle towns, samurai retainers were incapable of policing at the village level. Compared with many peasant societies,[20] Tokugawa peasants enjoyed considerable latitude for local political organizing.

There are also more purely social factors to consider. According to Anthony Oberschall, the more segmented the col-

19. Eric R. Wolf, *Peasants* (Englewood Cliffs, N.J., 1966), pp. 89–93.
20. Skocpol, *States and Social Revolutions*, p. 115.

lectivity and the more extensive and viable its communal ties, the greater its capabilities to mobilize.[21] Hence, the strenuous attempts by the Tokugawa shogun to enforce class distinctions which isolated peasants from the warrior and merchant classes had the unanticipated effect of enhancing their capacity to engage in collective action, since innumerable legal restrictions on occupation, residence, marriage, movement, and even public demeanor, food, and dress sharply differentiated peasants from all other classes.

Finally, one should note that, with few exceptions, Japanese peasants constituted a racially, ethnically, and linguistically homogeneous population; that no caste system divided villages into ritually and functionally discrete social groups; and that competing religions did not create exclusive and distrustful communities. Many of the structural barriers to mobilization relating to race, religion, and other non-class affiliations simply were not present in the Japanese case.

Goals and Ideology

If Tokugawa peasants mobilized frequently, what did they hope to achieve? Like peasants everywhere, they tended to be defensive in their actions. Most commonly, they opposed higher taxes and interference with rural commerce and commodity production, the issues that directly affected their livelihood. They also protested venal administration and arbitrary justice, collusion between fief officials and merchants, and appointment of unworthy headmen. Generally, peasants of vassal daimyo addressed their grievances to the lord of the domain or senior officials, and peasants of the Tokugawa territories addressed theirs to the Bakufu—the executive organ of the shogunate. Thus, the movements had specific goals which were related to the peasants' economic and political condition and represented conscious efforts to improve their situation. Using

21. Anthony Oberschall, *Social Conflict and Social Movements* (Englewood Cliffs, N.J., 1973), p. 129.

Landsberger's formulation of some of the theoretical dimensions of peasant movements, we see that they were more likely to be instrumental than expressive, and to be based on low socioeconomic status.[22] Other issues, such as religion and national politics, did not play a genuine, independent role.

The foregoing only begins to characterize the goals of the movements. To understand the form that collective action took, the specific content of the peasants' demands, and the strategies adopted, we need to know more about what they were defending and the beliefs and values that informed their actions. What, then, did peasants hope to achieve through political mobilization, and how did they justify resistance?

In the seventeenth century, when the Tokugawa political economy acquired its definitive shape and form, villages faced two different types of crises.[23] The first was periodic dearth due to climate-related crop failure. The second was an endemic condition: small cultivators were being driven off the land because, year in and year out, they could not produce enough rice to feed themselves and pay the lord's tax on the land they cultivated. In both cases villages petitioned the lord of the domain to exercise "benevolence" so that they, the petitioners, could "continue as farmers." In the case of unusually poor harvests, he was expected to demonstrate his commitment to benevolent rule (*jinsei*) by granting emergency aid (*osukui*); and, if high taxes were forcing economically marginal cultivators to abandon farming, he should lower tax quotas accordingly. Even when protest assumed illegal and violent forms, peasants used the same language to explain and justify their actions. As Irwin Scheiner argues most convincingly, mobilization by peasants in defiance of seigneurial authority flowed from the belief that the lord was obliged to heed appeals for tax reductions and relief: as tax-paying "honorable peasants" (*onbyakushō*), reciprocity existed between them and the governing daimyo.[24]

From even the brief discussion above, one can see that the

22. Landsberger, "Peasant Unrest," p. 57.
23. See chap. 2, below, the section "Examples from Fukushima."
24. Scheiner, "Benevolent Lords."

concept of benevolent rule was a central political value. Its key role, however, raises the question of its origins: the peasants' formal claim to seigneurial benevolence had no antecedent in pre-Tokugawa feudalism, and neither was it something borrowed from a foreign culture. A shortcoming of Scheiner's phenomenological analysis is that the ideal roles and role behavior associated with "benevolent lords" and "honorable peasants" in early Tokugawa peasant movements are givens; there is no explanation of how these particular norms (and not others) became socially dominant. They became dominant, I contend, because seigneurial benevolence was much more than a prescription for elite public morality, as in Chinese Confucianism. Rather, within the political economy of Tokugawa feudalism, seigneurial exploitation contained specific contradictions with respect to small cultivators which in the short run could only be resolved by regular administrative procedures to provide emergency aid and moderate tax extraction. Successful management of the landed economy required practical adjustments which later became ideologized as the praxis of "benevolent rule."

The linked concept of "continuing as farmers" originally referred to the socioeconomic status of small cultivators, rather than subsistence in the commonly understood meaning of avoiding starvation. It is important to note that in the early Tokugawa period "continuing as farmers" had a socially precise and restricted meaning which should not be subsumed under the more general normative concept of a "moral economy" of subsistence, which James Scott sees as the underlying ideology of peasant rebellions in southeast Asia.[25] Despite outward similarity, there are critical differences which account for the particular dynamic of Tokugawa peasant movements. The "moral economy" presumably includes all members of the community, regardless of socioeconomic status, and espouses the principle that no one shall starve so long as there are sufficient local resources to satisfy minimum consumption needs. In theory, it is inclusive of all "the poor," and the threshold of resistance which

25. James C. Scott, *The Moral Economy of the Peasant* (New Haven, Conn., 1976).

Scott predicts would ultimately correspond to socially defined levels of physical survival. If pushed below these thresholds by landlords or the state, peasants will rebel.[26] Compared with Scott's model, the norms that guided Tokugawa peasants were more restrictive but also set lower thresholds. At least in the early Tokugawa period, it was the fate of registered land-holders—not all peasants—that impelled collective action, and the threshold of resistance was solvency, rather than physical survival. That is, Tokugawa peasants tended to mobilize in opposition to seigneurial rule when increased taxes or poor harvests threatened to force a critical number of landholders to default on tax obligations. Peasants who failed to pay their portion of the tax lost legal title to the holdings and became "broken farmers" (tsuburebyakushō), forced to migrate or sell themselves as indentured servants. Due to the fact that the village was corporately liable for final payment of all feudal dues, the survival of small landholders was a matter of vital concern to peasants with middle-sized and large holdings.

Before turning to consideration of other aspects of Tokugawa peasant movements, I should like to extract from the above discussion the assumptions that informed peasants' collective action. First, as already stated, "benevolent rule" implied the obligation of the lord to protect, by means of judicious fiscal policies, the livings of small cultivators. Implicit in this conception was the assumption that the survival of peasant farmers was primarily a political question amenable to political solutions. The assumption was logical, given the economic realities of the subsistence agricultural economy in the early Tokugawa period: The size of the land tax was the primary determinant of peasants' well-being; and by timely adjustments the lord of the domain could save peasants from becoming "broken farmers" and, thereby, guarantee their socioeconomic status as primary producers. Second, there was the norm of obligatory collective action by villagers when crisis loomed. The entire community would join and bear the consequences; high-status

26. Ibid., pp. 7–8.

peasants would be expected to play an active role, even if they were personally immune from the immediate effects.

The ideology just described was the product of peasants' collective efforts in the seventeenth century to limit seigneurial exploitation and proved to be a valuable political resource in their unending struggle to retain a larger share of the fruits of their labor. One should not assume, however, that because it was politically effective, it was also radical, for the sociopolitical relationships implied by its principal normative constructs were doggedly conservative. As Fukaya Katsumi has demonstrated, the norms of benevolent rule and "continuing as farmers" corresponded to the objective needs of individual, small-scale cultivators in the subsistence economy of the early Tokugawa period.[27] Security of tenure was paramount, and peasants sought security within the existing status order by appealing to the ideal roles of lord and peasant. Although the ideal could be used to criticize the real, there was nothing in the ideology that was heretical; nothing that would impel peasants to go beyond the status definitions of the feudal polity.[28]

Collective Action and Violence

A salient feature of Tokugawa peasant movements was the low level of violence. Except at the beginning of the Tokugawa period, protests by peasants did not lead to bloody confrontation with the authorities whose policies they disputed. The rare resort to lethal force was itself the consequence of the asymmetrical power relationship that characterized social relations in the Tokugawa state. Like all governments, the Bakufu and the localized regimes of vassal daimyo "controlled the principal, concerted means of coercion within [the] population."[29] What was unusual, here, was the degree to which the seigneurial class mo-

27. Fukaya (n. 11 above), pp. 67–68.
28. Yasumaro Yoshi, *Nihon no kindaika to minshū shisō* (Tokyo, 1974), pp. 187–188.
29. Tilly, *From Mobilization to Revolution*, p. 125.

nopolized power. We have seen that in the late sixteenth and early seventeenth century warriors were settled in castle towns and the peasantry was disarmed, and that the policy of national isolation, by eliminating overseas trade and intercourse, reinforced the status quo. We should also consider the size and martial character of the ruling class. Samurai made up between five and seven percent of the population in most fiefs. All samurai males received military training, and shogun and daimyo maintained large standing armies which could be mobilized at a moment's notice. Because of the numerical strength and social character of the warrior aristocracy, shogun and daimyo did not need to conscript commoners or hire mercenaries. The morale, discipline, and commitment of the forces which could be used against peasants was correspondingly high; their service in time of need, unquestioned. Peasants, on the other hand, lacked training as well as arms and, barring defections from the ruling class, experienced leaders. The class structure and the policies of social control effectively denied them the use of armed force as a political resource.

Remembering Tilly's important observation that violence in conjunction with popular movements has historically been the result of repressive action initiated by the state, we may ask why the ruling class did not provoke armed clashes when peasants protested. The preceding analysis of the goals and ideological content of Tokugawa peasant movements provides at least part of the answer. The goals of these movements were specific, focused on issues such as taxes, aid, and officials' acts of malfeasance. Peasants bargained for limited improvements in the material conditions of their lives; they did not dispute the hegemonic position of the warrior class. Thus, the great restraint shown by feudal lords should be explained first of all as a realistic response to the perceived threat.

On the one occasion when peasants organized a revolutionary movement, the Shimabara rebellion, the response was entirely different. In 1637 peasants in Christianized districts of western Kyushu, near Nagasaki, who had suffered violent religious persecution and severe exploitation at the hands of an unusually rapacious lord, followed a youthful, self-proclaimed messiah in armed revolt against the feudal state. Led by village headmen and joined by *rōnin* (masterless samurai), between ten and twenty thousand peasants occupied an abandoned castle and fought for six months before being subdued. Entering the rebels' stronghold, the victorious samurai killed every man, woman, and child who had survived the siege. The seigneurial class, then, tolerated protest but was prepared to use maximum force against radical challenges to its authority.

In the latter half of the Tokugawa period peasant movements changed in certain important respects. To begin with, there was a great deal more of them. The number of protests rose from an average of 4.9 per year in the seventeenth century to 11.8 in the eighteenth century, and to 14.8 between 1800 and 1868.[30] Protests became larger and more disorderly. While illegal but peaceful appeals predominated in the early Tokugawa period, mass demonstrations accompanied by considerable destruction of property typified collective action in late Tokugawa. Although they did not take up arms and attempt to seize power in their own right, peasants had clearly become more aggressive and disputatious, and less in awe of the authority of their rulers.

How and why protests changed, and what the changes signified, are the problems to be analyzed in the chapters that follow. The assumption is that changes in peasant mobilization were the product of the growth of the market economy and changing relations *within* the peasant class due to dependency on the market and to capitalistic relations of production within rural society, for even when the Tokugawa hegemony collapsed, collective action by peasants was directed first and foremost against wealthy commoners rather than the ruling class. The frequency and intensity of peasant protests peaked at the time of the Meiji Restoration, but for the most part peasants were observers and not actors in the ensuing revolution.

30. Aoki, app., p. 34.

2. The Political Economy of Benevolence

The political economy of Tokugawa feudalism was built on the institutional innovations of Toyotomi Hideyoshi (1538–1598), the first warlord in more than two centuries to defeat or force peace on his major rivals. During his reign as hegemon, Hideyoshi created institutions which stabilized the feudal polity and revitalized the power of the warrior class. The key element in Hideyoshi's reforms was the physical separation of the warrior and peasant classes.[1] To understand why this solved the problem of chronic revolt and unrest, it is helpful to consider the particular problems of social control in the sixteenth century.

Since the decline of the Ashikaga shogunate in the fifteenth century, the absence of institutional controls over vassals had prevented warlords from consolidating power at the local level in the territories they conquered. By granting proprietary rights (*ryōshuken*) to retainers, daimyo ceded powers of local

---

1. The literature in Japanese on *heinō bunri* (separation of warrior and farmer) and the *kokudaka* system is vast, but one should make special note of the following: Araki Moriaki, *Bakuhan taisei no seiritsu to kōzō* (Tokyo, 1959); Asao Naohiro, *Kinsei hōken shakai no kiso kōzō* (Tokyo, 1967); Kitajima Masamoto, *Edo Bakufu no kenryoku kōzō* (Tokyo, 1959); and Sasaki Junnosuke, *Bakuhan kenryoku no kiso kōzō* (Tokyo, 1969). I am particularly indebted to Araki's brilliant (and controversial) study. In English see *Japan before Tokugawa*, ed. J. W. Hall, K. Nagahara, and K. Yamamura (Princeton, N.J., 1981), pp. 194–223, 271–294.

control which ultimately made their subordinates dangerously self-sufficient in the political realm. Vassals who acquired hereditary fiefs and warriors who enjoyed local rights of exploitation commanded economic and military resources which to varying degrees could be mobilized without the sanction of higher authority. Such power greatly diminished the need to render loyal service; not surprisingly, retainers frequently broke solemn oaths of fealty to gain greater power. Throughout the sixteenth century, vassals deserted daimyo, retainers betrayed lords, officers murdered generals, villages even rebelled against overlords. High status did not command the obedience of subordinates, and daimyo, if not fighting one another, were often busy preventing rebellions at home.[2]

Hideyoshi's genius was to see that removing samurai from the countryside and disarming villages solved the problem of betrayal and revolt. Earlier, the introduction of cannon and firearms from the West and construction of massive castles had forced daimyo to reorganize their retainers into standing armies and expand and centralize administrative powers, particularly those related to taxation. Hideyoshi went one step further, for he realized that only retainers directly dependent on their lords were likely to be truly loyal; therefore, the cutting of all links between the warrior class and the land was required. As he extended his rule in the late sixteenth century by defeating rivals and concluding alliances, Hideyoshi ordered samurai of all ranks to leave country strongholds and follow daimyo to centrally located castle towns.

The shogun Tokugawa Ieyasu (1542– 1616) and his successors completed the settlement of samurai in castle towns. They permitted daimyo to maintain only one castle and all retainers resided in its vicinity. Whether soldiers or administrators, henceforth samurai drew stipends from the lord's treasury, and

2. The collapse of central authority in the fifteenth century inaugurated a century of uninterrupted warfare conventionally dated 1467– 1576. The long-term cause was the decline of the influence of institutions and groups whose political and economic power was derived from the *shōen* (manorial) system: the Ashikaga shogunate, the Buddhist monastic orders, the emperor, and the court nobility.

the rice thus received was their sole source of support.[3] Daimyo were now able to watch closely over their retainers and reduce or cancel stipends at the first sign of insubordination, which they did with impunity since retainers no longer lived in distant villages and rural redoubts. Likewise, shogun-dominated vassal daimyo, limited to a single castle, could not hope to withstand Bakufu armies. Before long every aspect of their political life was regulated from above and samurai at last exhibited the absolute loyalty traditionally ascribed to the Japanese warrior.

The disarming of the peasantry, the second of Hideyoshi's contributions to the revitalization of the feudal order, flowed naturally from the removal of samurai to castle towns. Village chiefs and large landowners posed special problems with respect to local control. Although farmers rather than professional samurai, during the long period of near anarchy in the fifteenth and sixteenth centuries they had taken up arms in self-defense. Their large households included collateral relatives and hereditary servants who made up a potential fighting force. In the sixteenth century these powerful peasant families had joined local campaigns and fought alongside warriors; in some areas they even formed leagues to resist warlords.[4] Armed villagers were not likely to be obedient subjects, especially after the departure of samurai, and in 1588 Hideyoshi ordered a nationwide "sword hunt" to remove both firearms and traditional weapons from the countryside. That peasants did not lose their weapons all at once was demonstrated by the Shimabara rebellion in 1637/38, but armed resistance by them, not uncommon in the sixteenth and early seventeenth centuries, ceased after 1650.

Hideyoshi's third institutional innovation, the *kokudaka* system of fief registers, is discussed in greater detail below with specific reference to peasants' protests, and we earlier observed that the new, bureaucratic procedures for assessing land rents permitted daimyo to tax peasants without directly overseeing

3. See chap. 1, above, n. 12.
4. David Davis, "*Ikki* in Late Medieval Japan," *Medieval Japan*, ed. J. W. Hall and J. P. Mass (New Haven, Conn., 1974), pp. 221–247.

the landed economy. In theory, officials in possession of detailed and up-to-date records of village land productivity and
population could assess the annual land tax without leaving the
castle town, and served the needs of the urbanized ruling class
by minimizing samurai supervision. But the new land registers
also profoundly altered the village status order by raising formerly dependent families to the status of independent cultivators and reducing the authority of the large proprietor class.[5]
Comparing the new system of land registration with prior arrangements will show how this happened.

Before Hideyoshi's reforms, only high-status peasants held
title to land, and they paid taxes directly to the overlord. This
elite class of proprietors (*myōshu*) controlled extensive holdings
which they farmed by mobilizing family members, collateral
relatives, nonrelated dependents, and hereditary servants.[6] By
the sixteenth century, however, the *myōshu* generally did not
cultivate all of their "name holdings" themselves, especially in
highly productive villages in the Kinai region where they
granted cultivating rights to families who became sharecrop-
pers. In less developed regions, the dependent families were
tied more closely to the main house, though they, too, gradually
acquired customary rights to certain parcels of farmland and,
in some cases, separate dwellings. Regardless of the degree of
economic independence, however, these peasants remained
subject to the authority of the proprietor, who as the registered
holder paid all of the dues demanded by the overlord.

This pattern of landholding allowed large proprietors to exercise considerable power by virtue of their position as intermediaries between lord and peasant, thereby diluting the

5. Araki, *Bakuhan taisei*, argues that the historical significance of the surveys and the *kokudaka* system is to be found in the rise of the small-family cultivator and the decline of the large or extended family system of unfree labor
(*tezukuri*) organized under elite proprietors (*myōshu*). Some scholars question
Araki's interpretation, as in J. W. Hall, "Hideyoshi's Domestic Politics," in *Japan
before Tokugawa*, ed. J. W. Hall, K. Nagahara, and K. Yamamura (Princeton, N.J.,
1981), pp. 211–218.

6. The semimartial, large-scale proprietors were also called *dogō, gōshi*,
and *jizamurai*.

lord's fiscal and political authority. Nevertheless, the system served the needs of daimyo, since in the sixteenth century they were constantly at war and most of their retainers were self-supporting. Often the daimyo most pressingly needed not money but food, horses, and peasants' labor to build fortifications and transport supplies. Rather than mobilize thousands of small landholders, they preferred to call on the chief households who directly controlled local resources.

By the end of the sixteenth century the needs of the daimyo had changed dramatically. Samurai living in castle towns required stipends, which greatly increased demands on the lord's treasury. In order to increase output and the rate of tax extraction, Hideyoshi's land surveys recorded the names of individual peasants and the plots they customarily farmed. Once entered on the tax rolls, these peasants became the legal landholders. Thus the tax system paid double dividends, first by allowing daimyo to tax directly the small peasant farmers, and second by reducing the power of the large proprietor class which had formerly dominated these peasants. Peasants listed in the early surveys became known as *honbyakushō* (main peasants). To keep the status and rights of proprietorship, they had to pay the onerous land tax and other dues apportioned according to the size of registered holdings. Most did. By the end of the seventeenth century, *honbyakushō* made up the majority in most villages.

The size and strength of the *honbyakushō* class increased throughout the seventeenth century due to a variety of other circumstances through which formerly landless peasants acquired cultivating rights. First, as rear vassals and country samurai (*jizamurai*) moved to castle towns, the peasants who had farmed their fields became the legal holders.[7] Second, in many areas daimyo and the Bakufu reclaimed extensive new land which the peasants later settled. In the third case, the main household released part of its holdings in order to establish

7. Whether samurai joined the lord's corps of retainers *(kashindan)* ·or stayed in the village affected the pattern of landholding since if they departed the distribution of land was likely to be more nearly equal than if they stayed. Hirasawa Kyoto, *Kinsei sonraku no ikō to heinō bunri* (Tokyo, 1973).

branch houses. The reasons for dividing the patrimony varied, as did the specific arrangements,[8] but the new tax system and increased production for the market appear to have played the major role. Because of higher taxes and the shift from labor services to rents, proprietors with very large holdings found it advantageous to give up smaller and less productive parcels. The branch household now paid the land tax, which was likely to be high; but small families farming their own land had greater incentives to squeeze the most out of the holdings.[9] Growth of urban markets and technological changes toward more labor-intensive methods also encouraged the formation of smaller farming units, which, as Thomas Smith has shown, proved to be better suited to the more complex demands on the work force.[10]

By the end of the seventeenth century, small farm families had become the dominant social group in the countryside. In analyzing the changes in the village, it is important to recognize the separate, though complementary, contributions made to the evolving Tokugawa village by the new system of land rents and economic and demographic trends. The institutional relationships established by the *kokudaka* system were generally the same everywhere and were fully developed by the middle of the seventeenth century. The growth of the economy and population, however, were gradual processes which varied greatly with regional factors. Specifically, the size and strength of the small peasant class depended on land endowment, access to fertilizer and water, proximity to markets, and many other factors likely to effect labor productivity. Where productivity was high, the small peasant class tended to be numerically large and economically secure, and where low, to be fewer in number and weaker. In less-developed regions, many small peasants continued to

8. Usually the holdings of the main house *(honke)* were considerably larger than those of branch houses *(bekke)*. But sometimes the division appeared to be nearly equal, as in parts of Aizu. Yamada Shun, *Nihon hōken sei no kōzō bunseki* (Tokyo, 1956), p. 57.

9. Araki, *Bakuhan taisei*, pp. 215–217.

10. Thomas C. Smith, *Agrarian Origins of Modern Japan* (Stanford, Calif., 1959), pp. 140–156.

depend on large landholders, exchanging labor for land, draft animals, compost, and seed, and some continued to live in the compound of the main house. The status of such families was only slightly higher than that of hereditary servants and indentured laborers.

Even allowing for regional differences in the size of the *honbyakushō* class, the policies of removing samurai from the countryside, disarming villages, and instituting the *kokudaka* system created a new order in rural Japan characterized by a profound leveling of social and economic status. Instead of settlements organized socially and economically under the familial authority of elite proprietors and country warriors, Tokugawa villages were typically composed of several large and many small farmers whose legal status and obligations as landholders were fixed by the new institutional relationship to higher authority. Status varied, of course. The elite possessed most of the land and served as headmen. Some became chief headmen who supervised as many as ten or twenty villages. To encourage their cooperation, daimyo granted various perquisites and status privileges—partial tax exemptions, small stipends, surnames, and ceremonial swords. But they were not samurai. Like ordinary peasants they were commoners and subject to the laws and demands of shogun and daimyo.

Conflict over the Land Tax

Data on peasant movements after the adoption of the new system show how completely disputes over tax assessments dominated class relations in the early Tokugawa period. Aoki Kōji has identified the primary causes of 381 rural protests and uprisings against seigneurial authority between 1590 and 1699.[11] Peasants voiced many different complaints: extortion, embezzlement, famine, corvée, exporting rice, withholding aid, sur-

11. Aoki Kōji, *Hyakushō ikki no nenjiteki kenkyū* (Tokyo, 1966), pp. 41–45. Intravillage disputes *(murakata sōdō)* are not included, nor are conflicts where the cause could not be determined.

charges, overcharging, arbitrary demands, harsh and violent rule. But protests against land surveys, 34 cases (9 percent), and high assessments, 126 cases (33 percent), overshadow all others. Of course, classifying causes and counting cases does not measure the scale, duration, or intensity of the movements. Nevertheless, the fact that land surveys and higher assessments triggered so many of the protests during the first century of Tokugawa rule shows that the new system of exploitation galvanized peasant opposition.

The increased rate of tax extraction in the seventeenth century was due entirely to exhaustive cadastral surveys. Officials visited each village in the fief, classified the general quality of its arable land, and measured and rated each parcel of irrigated (paddy) and unirrigated land. Next they selected several top paddy fields and, if possible, harvested a portion of the crop. The projected yield of the top-grade rice fields less deductions for seed and spoilage determined the *kokumori*—the rating per *tan* (.245 acre), measured in *koku* of rice.[12] Lower ratings were assigned to dry fields and less productive parcels of paddy. Totaling data on size and ratings produced an estimate of land productivity called the *kokudaka*. The tax rate was expressed as the percentage of the *kokudaka;* it varied but in most fiefs ranged from 40 to 60 percent. Some fiefs inspected crops before the harvest and adjusted the tax rate accordingly, while in others it was fixed. The land tax made up the bulk of the village's taxes. In principle, taxes were paid in *koku* of rice, but many fiefs permitted peasants to commute up to half of the tax at a fixed rate of exchange. Additional taxes were assessed on nonagricultural products such as paper, charcoal, timber, fish, silk, wax, and lacquer. At first these taxes were collected in kind; later many were commuted.

The *kokudaka* system made it possible for daimyo to tax land directly and, in theory, at a rate calculated to leave only enough

12. The standard schedule rated top-grade paddy at 1.5 *to* per *tan*, and each lower grade 0.2 *to* less (1.0 *to* = 4.76 gallons; 1.0 *tan* = 0.245 acres). Dry fields were generally rated 0.2 *to* less than the corresponding grade of paddy. *Shinpan gōshi shi jiten*, ed. Ōtsuka Shigakkai (Tokyo, 1969), pp. 191–193.

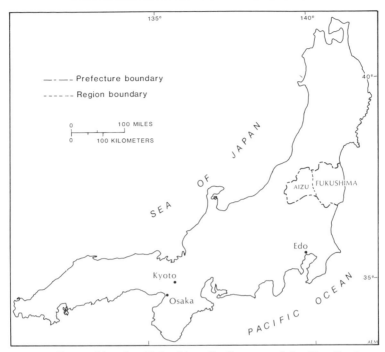

MAP 1. *Japan, Showing Fukushima Prefecture and the Aizu Region*

grain for peasants to subsist on from one year to the next. As indicated by Tokugawa Ieyasu's often quoted instructions to his intendants that peasants be taxed to the point where they could neither live nor die, the intent was to expropriate the entire surplus.[13] Extant data matching output and tax collection are extremely scarce, however, and how close the seigneurial class came to realizing the professed goal cannot be said. As critics of the

13. Most Japanese historians argue that until the end of the seventeenth century, when the seigneurial class switched from the *kemi* (on-site) to the *jōmen* (fixed-rate) system, tax extraction approached expropriation of the entire surplus. There are some data to support this argument: Sasaki Junnosuke, "Kinsei nōson no seiritsu," *Iwanami kōza Nihon rekishi,* vol. 10 (Tokyo, 1963), pp. 165–221; but with a few exceptions (pp. 171–172) the data only give tax revenue and not the *rate* of tax extraction.

"total expropriation" thesis have observed, higher productivity due to expansion of arable land, improved technology, and more intensive labor inputs undoubtedly benefited cultivators.[14] Unless the daimyo were unusually vigilant in ordering new surveys and updating ratings, peasants retained at least part of the increase in output. Moreover, the procedures used to estimate productivity, which were highly accurate in the case of rice, tended to underestimate the value of cash crops. The prosperity of peasants in cotton-producing districts of western Japan provides evidence to this effect. But while the economic data are ambiguous, the intention was clearly to maximize revenue.

Examples from Fukushima

Toyotomi Hideyoshi carried out the first comprehensive surveys of Fukushima in 1590. Victory at Odawara had eliminated his major rivals in the northeast, and Hideyoshi ordered land surveys to consolidate control over the region. A letter sent to the chief surveyor, Asano Nagamasa, expressed his concern that the job be done thoroughly. Asano was urged to be as methodical as possible, covering one district at a time, surveying even deserted villages and fallow fields, penetrating deep into mountain valleys and knee-deep into the sea; if he should tire, Hideyoshi jokingly threatened to finish the job himself. Nevertheless, the scale of the undertaking was enormous, the time short, and the first survey was necessarily a rough affair. A subsequent survey begun in 1594, raised the *kokudaka* by 20 percent, from 734,270 *koku* to 919,320.[15]

In the Shindatsu district of Fukushima, frequent surveys during the seventeenth century raised productivity estimates substantially. A survey in 1615 added 10 percent, and subsequent surveys 27 percent. The fourth and last comprehensive

14. Susan Hanley and Kozo Yamamura, *Economic and Demographic Change in Premodern Japan* (Princeton, N.J., 1977), pp. 19–28.

15. *Aizu-Wakamatsu shi,* vol. 2 (Aizu-Wakamatsu, 1965), pp. 34–35, 47.

MAP 2. *Fukushima Prefecture in the Tokugawa Period*

survey, executed in 1664, raised the total to 196,850 *koku*.[16] In seventy-five years the *kokudaka* increased nearly 80 percent. Land under cultivation also increased because of numerous reclamation projects. Thus the data can be read variously. Perhaps the higher *kokudaka* merely recorded newly cultivated land and did not indicate a higher rate of tax extraction; perhaps the surveyors uncovered "hidden fields" and raised the ratings of old fields, which enabled the lord to claim a higher proportion of the crop. But by either account, in contrast to the sixteenth century, when daimyo rarely updated tax rolls, in the seventeenth century the seigneurial class used surveys aggressively to prevent peasants from accumulating wealth—a goal that Confucian moralists applauded as enthusiastically as the treasurer of the daimyo.

16. *Fukushima-shi shi*, vol. 2 (Fukushima, 1972), pp. 210–213.

In an early petition, dated 1625, the headman of Ishimo-chiri village in Nihonmatsu petitioned against increased village quotas for corvée labor which had been ordered by the fief.

> The labor quota of our village . . . has been raised from six to seventeen men, and this is causing the greatest difficulty to farmers. Every year some must sell their daughters just to keep from losing their land. Even so, four of the eleven farmers have been reduced to landless peasants.[17]

The headman argued that the seven remaining households could not possibly fill the new quota and warned that "only if you hear this appeal and order reductions will we be able to live as peasants."

The petition from Ishimochiri dates from the transitional period in which corvée labor constituted a significant portion of the charges levied on villages. There is no record of how the daimyo of Nihonmatsu responded, but in most fiefs labor services were reduced and commuted to cash payments by the mid-seventeenth century. One reason was the decline in public works projects and military service to the Bakufu.[18] But daimyo also wished to expand the tax base by promoting small peasant farmers, and corvée labor was particularly burdensome to the newly registered peasants who depended entirely on family members to cultivate their holdings.[19] In economic terms, labor services were "lumpy," and if the period of service overlapped with labor peaks in agriculture, the result could be disastrous. In the case of Ishimochiri, a third of the peasant farmers, presumably newly registered holders, had been forced to indenture themselves, thus losing their land and status as *hyakushō*— peasant farmers.

Commuting labor services aided the small proprietor, but if daimyo pushed too hard in raising assessments the results were

17. *Tōhoku shohan hyakushō ikki no kenkyū: Shiryō shūsei*, ed. Shōji Kichinosuke (Tokyo, 1969), pp. 478–479; hereafter cited as *Tōhoku ikki*.
18. Sasaki Junnosuke, "Bakuhan taisei no kōzōteki tokushitsu," *Ronshū Nihon shi*, vol. 7, ed. Odachi Uki (Tokyo, 1973), pp. 1–15.
19. Araki, *Bakuhan taisei*, pp. 86–87.

the same. Early in the spring of 1700, sixteen headmen and three assistant headmen from the Shindatsu district petitioned the Bakufu magistrate in protest against increasing taxes. They complained that since 1664 the government had on two occasions assigned their villages to daimyo only to reverse the decision a few years later and resume direct rule. The headmen did not indicate whether they preferred daimyo or Bakufu officials, but protested that each administration carried out new cadastral surveys. The surveys added previously unregistered fields to village tax rolls and raised the *kokudaka* ratings of old fields. "The land tax has increased sixty, seventy, even a hundred percent," they complained, "causing great hardship to farmers." They pointed out that their villages had experienced unusually bad weather in the spring and summer, with damaging consequences. "Most peasant proprietors are in danger of losing their land . . . and without emergency loans of seed and rice cannot even plant next year's crop." The headmen made two requests: First, that the land tax be reduced to what it had been thirty-five years earlier; and second, that the government provide loans of rice and seed to tide them over until the next harvest. They closed with an urgent appeal that the government act to "restore the condition of landholding peasants that they may continue as farmers."[20]

Although the poorest peasants were the first to default, onerous taxes affected the entire village and even prosperous peasants had reason to fear the consequences. In 1712, peasants from Nakahata village, Shirakawa, submitted a petition in which they complained that four times in the past thirty-four years officials had carried out new cadastral surveys. Each survey produced a higher assessment of the village's productivity and consequently higher taxes. Many peasants with small and unfertile holdings could not pay what the fief now demanded. Thirty years earlier the village had had nine hundred residents, but rising taxes had "broken" (*tsubure*) many small proprietors who, unable to pay, forfeited their land rights. At the time of the petition, the population had shrunk to 712, and of this

20. *Tōhoku ikki*, p. 258.

number 87 were landless peasants who had been forced to indenture themselves to wealthy peasants in nearby villages.[21]

The declining number of peasant farmers in Nakahata added to the tax burden on the village's solvent farmers. Although the land registers recorded each family's holdings and taxes, under the *kokudaka* system the village was liable for taxes assessed on registered fields whether or not cultivated that year; consequently land abandoned by broken farmers became a corporate charge. One solution was to find new tenants, but if the village was losing population, as in Nakahata, this was not easy to do. The peasants complained: "Even though we parcel out this land to new farming households, landless farmers, and even to the aged, this spring there are still thirty-eight *koku* of land that no one will farm." Uncultivated land meant even higher taxes for the remaining landholders and set off a cycle of abandoned land, population decline, and higher taxes. The peasants therefore asked the Bakufu to discontinue new surveys and suspend, for three years, taxes currently assessed on abandoned land. The petition emphasized that these concessions would ultimately benefit the government. "From the fourth year the new farmers will pay taxes assessed on the land and will be able to farm it for many generations." It closed with a strong plea for "benevolent consideration so that we can continue forever as peasants of the domain."[22]

Petitioning for tax reductions was the first line of defense in villages where excessive dues threatened to break small farm families. In addition to providing evidence of the effects of the taxes, the petitions reveal the rhetorical strategy peasants used to persuade officials of the reasonableness and justice of their demands. The argument was economic and rational. Each petition closed with a set phrase that they, the petitioners, be able to "continue as farmers" (*hyakushō aitsuzuki*).[23] In the predominantly agricultural economy of Tokugawa Japan, the labor of thousands

21. Ibid., pp. 541–542.
22. Ibid., p. 542.
23. Fukaya Katsumi, *Hyakushō ikki no rekishiteki kōzō* (Tokyo, 1979), pp. 65–66.

of small proprietors supported the lord and his house men, making the fief financially dependent on the survival (though not the prosperity) of farmers who, year after year, paid charges on registered fields. As we have seen, petitioners made pointed references to "broken farmers" to evoke the specter of abandoned rice fields and underpopulated villages. The moral did not need to be spelled out. When ruinous taxes drove peasants off the land, there were soon more registered fields than people to farm them. If the lord did not restore the balance, the decline in cultivated land reduced tax revenues and ultimately jeopardized the fiscal stability of the fief.

Daimyo Bad and Good:
Aizu in the Seventeenth Century

The rule of the daimyo Katō Yoshiaki and his son Akinari was turbulent and short. Yoshiaki entered Aizu fief in 1627 and soon contracted a fatal disease which incapacitated him until his death in 1631. Akinari, who succeeded his father, was a brave soldier. He had distinguished himself some years earlier fighting for Tokugawa Ieyasu at the siege of Osaka castle, but was impetuous and indiscreet and made enemies at the shogun's court. In 1643, sixteen years after his father's entry into Aizu, the Bakufu charged Akinari with disloyal conduct and confiscated the fief, bringing the Katō line to an abrupt and ignominious end.[24]

Although not specifically mentioned in the five-article indictment handed down against Akinari, peasant unrest in Aizu contributed to the downfall of the Katō house. Discontent with the new administration surfaced almost immediately. Soon after entering Aizu, Yoshiaki ordered a land survey and authorized new procedures for assessing and collecting taxes. Instead of the three-grade classification system, the Katō survey used ten grades and substantially increased productivity esti-

24. *Aizu-Wakamatsu shi*, vol. 2, pp. 136–138.

mates.[25] Hastily executed, the Katō survey produced wild discrepancies between actual and assessed productivity: In the extreme case taxes were assessed on totally barren land, and thriving populations attributed to abandoned villages. Playing on a calligraphic pun, peasants made sarcastic reference to the Katō *mayoidaka*, "wandering assessments."[26] They objected to the procedures used to measure the volume and quality of rice paid as taxes, and also were burdened by new taxes on cotton cloth, firewood, and various local products.

The fiscal policies of the Katō administration weighed heavily on the peasants of Aizu, who after fifteen years of unrelenting tax pressure suffered severely in 1642 and 1643 when crop failures afflicted much of the country. Memories of the recent Shimabara uprising (1637/38) made the Bakufu particularly sensitive to the prospect of peasant revolts, and in the autumn of 1642 it took the unprecedented step of issuing instructions urging daimyo to show special consideration to peasants, warning that it would not look favorably on harsh and unjust rule at a time of imminent famine.[27]

Despite the Bakufu's admonitions, Aizu officials did little to ameliorate the plight of the peasants. Discontented with the administration and perhaps influenced by the Bakufu's pronouncements, several thousand peasants joined *chōsan ikki*, organized flights by many if not all of the peasants in a particular village, which took place in the closing months of 1642.[28]

Unlike solitary and secret departures by individual families, most *chōsan ikki* were protests designed to win concessions by arousing public opinion. Led by the village headman, peasants harvested their crops, packed up belongings, and fled en masse to neighboring domains. Once across the border, they com-

---

25. Itō Tasaburō, "Kinsei daimyo kenkyū josetsu," pt. 2, *Shigaku zasshi* 57 (November 1944): 1173. E.g., the Katō *kokumori* rating of top-grade paddy was 1.7 *to*, compared with the old rating of 1.4 *to*, while top dry field was rated 1.6 *to*, compared with 0.7 *to*.
26. *Aizu-Wakamatsu shi*, vol. 2, p. 154.
27. Ibid., pp. 157–158.
28. Ibid., p. 158.

plained loudly and petitioned the Bakufu to come to their aid. Although prepared to settle elsewhere if protest failed, they returned if the lord granted their demands.

Hoping to effect a quick settlement and forestall Bakufu intervention, Akinari canceled 3,500 *ryō* owed in back taxes. The peasants, however, appear to have been more impressed by the rewards he offered for their capture, and few volunteered to return. As noted earlier, the following spring the Bakufu confiscated Akinari's fief.

Two months after Katō Akinari's indictment the shogun appointed Hoshina Masayuki (1611–1672) daimyo of Aizu. It was unlikely that Masayuki would repeat the mistakes of his predecessor. Five years earlier he had witnessed a rebellion by the peasants of Shiraiwa fief which demonstrated the high costs of despotic rule. Long oppressed by heavy taxes and harsh laws, the peasants stormed the castle town and killed a senior fief official. Sent to help restore order, Masayuki saw the Bakufu execute a hundred and thirty peasants *and* confiscate the fief in line with its policy of chastising daimyo who provoked peasant unrest.[29]

A bumper harvest in 1643 eliminated the immediate cause of peasants' distress in Aizu, and after entering the domain Masayuki instituted changes in administration which helped to restore the prosperity of the rural economy. Some of the reforms were essentially coercive: Peasants were forced to join five- and ten-household neighborhood associations and assume collective responsibility for cultivating members' fields, paying taxes, and filling corvée labor assignments.[30] The associations were instructed to prevent member households from absconding; if they failed, the associations were fined and held liable for payment of taxes on the abandoned land. Finally, village headmen were ordered to prepare detailed population registers to provide a higher degree of accountability.

Most daimyo in the early Tokugawa period employed similar

29. Itō (see n. 25, above), pt. 1, *Shigaku zasshi* 55 (September 1944): 936.
30. *Aizu-Wakamatsu shi*, vol. 3 (1965), p. 9.

measures to tie peasants to the land. Unlike many of his contemporaries, however, Masayuki realized that without constructive reforms, edicts binding peasants to the land often proved to be ineffectual. It should be emphasized that his reforms were not intended to reduce overall taxation, but to ensure that taxes be assessed as fairly as possible and with due attention to long-term effects.

First, Masayuki discontinued the complicated ratings used by the Katō daimyo and ordered new surveys to correct past errors. Begun in 1648, Masayuki's survey reassessed the fields of 179 villages and reduced the estimates by 13,000 *koku*.[31] In addition, 7,000 *koku* of land made barren by floods and landslides were struck from village registers. Second, he issued detailed regulations specifying the procedures to be used by district officials when measuring and grading the rice that peasants paid as taxes in kind. He also simplified taxes on cash crops, handicrafts, and special products. Only a few of the taxes were eliminated; they were, however, made part of the village *kokudaka* and were collected at the same time as the land tax, which put a halt to overcharging by tax officers.[32]

A second aspect of Masayuki's reforms was the granting of tax reductions and loans to protect small proprietors against default due to harvest shortfalls. Villages that suffered crop failure were encouraged to petition the district magistrates, who forwarded the information to senior officers in the castle town. In particularly bad years, the fief granted uniform reductions to all villages. But the greatest need was to protect peasants whose limited resources made them particularly vulnerable to natural disasters. The intent of the policy is clearly shown in the following instructions sent in 1663 to the district magistrates:

> The tax rate for the poorest villages should be reduced to 39 percent in order to help those whose need is greatest and prevent peasants who might otherwise default from being forced to become indentured servants. But exemptions should not be made where the

31. Itō, pt. 2, p. 1174.
32. Ibid.

village is strong. All dispensations should be made in accordance with this principle, no matter how great.[33]

It was not easy for officials to determine how much tax relief was needed, for the fief did not have the manpower to investigate each village's claim as to the condition of individual proprietors. Yet when officials made decisions on granting or denying requests for aid they did so on a village-by-village basis. There was always the risk, from the lord's point of view, that some peasants would profit. Consequently, district officers were constantly enjoined to make careful discriminations:

> The lord is pleased at the betterment of the peasants. Recently, however, peasants have been much given to buying *kosode* [padded silk garments] for weddings and such occasions. This must be stopped before it comes to the attention of the lord. Thus, it is important to make careful calculations, raising the rate for strong villages and lowering it for weak.[34]

In 1655 Masayuki went one step further and established a system of funding agencies (*shasō sei*). According to the charter, district officers were authorized to make loans to villagers in need of emergency assistance. Some of the loans were free, but the usual practice was to charge 20 percent interest—less than half the rate demanded by village moneylenders. Profits were returned to the fund, which also sponsored land reclamation and irrigation projects. In addition, it extended loans to new proprietors to encourage them to settle on the land.[35]

In time Masayuki came to be known as an "enlightened ruler" whose benevolent protection of his subjects was celebrated by Confucian moralists. Masayuki himself was a dedicated student of Confucianism and wrote several treatises on philosophy and statecraft. Benevolent rule—the obligation of the head of state to give first consideration to the welfare of his subjects—was a key Confucian norm, and there was an un-

33. Takagi Shōsaku, "Bakuhan taisei daiichi dankai kara daini dankai e no suikō ni tsuite," *Ronshū Nihon rekishi*, vol. 7 (Tokyo, 1973), p. 200.
34. Ibid., p. 201.
35. Ibid., pp. 205–206.

mistakable connection between Masayuki's policies as ruler of Aizu and Confucian principles of governance.

Yet the economic rationality of seigneurial policies of benevolent rule should not be overlooked, for the lord benefited to the extent that he increased the number of small peasant farmers.[36] As noted earlier, given the same resources, peasants were likely to work harder and more productively as small-scale subsistence farmers than as subordinate members of the households of large proprietors. When these small peasants became registered landholders and economically independent farmers, the lord taxed them directly. Moreover, they were then free to marry and raise children, which probably contributed to the rapid population growth of the early Tokugawa period. Given the high rate of tax extraction, however, these newly established peasant farmers were particularly vulnerable to crop failure and famine; without aid in the form of tax reductions and loans, they soon became "broken farmers," forced to migrate or sell themselves as indentured laborers. Seigneurial benevolence was needed to allow them to continue as farmers.

There is no doubt that Masayuki and his successors achieved the dual goal of protecting small proprietors and increasing fief tax revenues. Between the middle and the end of the seventeenth century, collection of tax rice rose 12 percent and population 24 percent, with the result that the average per capita tax fell from 0.90 *koku* to 0.81 *koku*.[37] Moreover, land reclamation—the fief granted loans and tax exemptions to peasants as incentives—added 23,000 *koku* of new land to the tax rolls in the period between Masayuki's accession in 1642 and 1680.[38] This was 3,000 *koku* more than the reduction initially ordered to correct the "wandering" assessments of the Katō survey.

36. Takagi Shōsaku argues this point, using Hoshina Masayuki as an example of the need for active intervention of the seigneurial class to protect newly registered peasant farmers. His article contributed substantially to my understanding of this problem.

37. Yamazaki Ryūzō, "Edo kōki ni okeru nōson keizai no hatten to nōminsō no bunkai," in *Iwanami kōza Nihon rekishi*, vol. 12 (Tokyo, 1963), p. 342.

38. Itō (n. 25 above), pt. 2, p. 1176.

Although only one particularly dramatic example of how "benevolence" sustained the seigneurial political economy, the contrast between the failure of the Katō family and the success of Hoshina and his successors illustrates an essential point: In the long run, single-minded pursuit of profit proved self-defeating, for the closer the lord came to eliminating the surplus, the greater was the risk of small proprietors' defaulting and absconding or, in the extreme case, revolting. If oppressive taxes drove peasants off the land, the lord lost future claims to the fruits of their labor; if they protested too loudly and long, he might even lose his domain.

A basic paradox of rule in the seventeenth century was that the confiscatory nature of the *kokudaka* system made benevolence a necessary function of fief administration. Because of fluctuations in yields and periodic crop failure, peasants could not survive without judicious adjustments in fiscal policy, and benevolence appeared to protect the interests of both lord and peasant. We should not be surprised to see that peasants began to demand benevolence, and that lords found it difficult to refuse.

3. Collective Action in the First Half of the Tokugawa Period

The Tokugawa ruling class severely restricted political activity by peasants. Banding together, distributing circulars, and staging demonstrations were strictly forbidden, and harsh penalties were prescribed to dissuade potential offenders. Peasants were, however, allowed to petition. In principle, only the headman could petition. Whether or not this peasant official was the actual author of a petition, he signed and deposited it at the district office (*daikansho*) nearest to the village. The intendant (*daikan*) examined the document and perhaps investigated. If satisfied as to the content and form, he forwarded it to the capital, where senior officials decided what action, if any, was advisable.

The shogun and daimyo permitted written appeals because the petitioning process opened a much-needed channel of communication between distant villages and the seat of domain authority. The information often proved useful. Appeals for special dispensation because of crop failure alerted authorities to impending food shortages; and complaints against local officials helped in controlling corruption among the low-status, poorly paid samurai who collected taxes and administered in the countryside.[1] Although slow and uncertain, the exchange

1. Kodama Kōta, *Kinsei nōmin seikatsu shi* (Tokyo, 1963), pp. 9–10. The Bakufu early recognized that extortion and overcharging by intendants was a cause of peasant unrest, and in the 1633 code permitted appeals to higher au-

of information and services initiated by peasants' petitions was essential to efficient administration; indeed, sooner or later every village found occasion to make appeals.

Not all petitions were welcome, and some were illegal. Insisting that fiscal policy was an exclusive prerogative, rulers refused to accept petitions protesting land surveys and high taxes. As early as 1586, Toyotomi Hideyoshi published edicts which threatened severe punishment in such cases, and, not long after, crucified seven peasants who violated the law.[2] Troubled by frequent protests against land surveys and high assessments, in 1633 the Bakufu declared that illegal petitions constituted a capital offense and advised strict adherence to rules of precedence, warning that peasants should not apply to higher authorities without first making appeals to district magistrates.[3]

Petitions against taxes closely resembled appeals for aid; in both cases the peasants used deferential language, warned of imminent disaster, and pleaded for benevolence so that they might continue as farmers. Moreover, the long-term effects of excessive taxation were similar to the short-term consequences of crop failure—both threatened to bankrupt small farmers. Whatever the cause, the phenomenon of "broken farmers" being forced out of the village sapped the vitality of the landed economy from which daimyo drew their revenue. Why, then, did they accept appeals for aid when crops failed but adamantly refuse to hear appeals for lower taxes?

Of course, ideology was one factor, since feudal lords may feel perfectly comfortable acting the role of benefactor to the long-suffering populace while rarely tolerating dissent. There

---

thority when peasants could not obtain satisfaction at the district level. Kimura Motoi, "Chōsan to utae," *Iwanami kōza Nihon rekishi,* vol. 10 (Tokyo, 1975), p. 228.

2. Hayashi Motoi, *Hyakushō ikki no dentō* (Tokyo, 1971), p. 5.

3. As with sumptuary laws and edicts legislating monopoly rights, the frequent issuing of laws prohibiting illegal petitions attests to their lack of efficacy. On the whole, fief laws followed those of the Bakufu. For a comparison of edicts issued by the Bakufu and Morioka fief between the late seventeenth and nineteenth century, see Fukaya Katsumi, "Hyakushō ikki," *Iwanami kōza Nihon rekishi,* vol. 11 (Tokyo, 1976), pp. 130–131.

were, however, practical reasons why daimyo refused to hear appeals for permanent tax reductions. Officials had little difficulty verifying peasants' claims of distress caused by natural disasters; a trained observer could accurately estimate the approximate extent of the damage caused by floods, frost, and drought.[4] Some villages suffered more than others, but a single tour might suffice to determine where aid was needed and how much. On the other hand, complaints that even in normal years taxes were too high entailed problems of verification beyond the competence of the administrative apparatus. Unlike wasted fields and stunted crops, population loss associated with "broken farmers" could not be measured until after permanent harm had been done to the villages. Never knowing when peasants exaggerated, daimyo tried to avoid being put in the position of acting on petitions whose claims they could not verify. Moreover, even in the same district there were strong and weak villages, and tax increases which the former could absorb, the latter could not. It was not practical to set different tax rates for each village—such would be an administrative nightmare. Rather, bureaucratic efficiency required setting uniform tax rates, rates which could be adjusted in any given year to accommodate harvest shortfalls, but which if lowered on every occasion that peasants protested might entail unacceptable loss of revenue.

The constraints on benevolence, therefore, were institutional and operated regardless of the good intentions and sincerity of the lord of the domain. Energetic and well-administered policies of loans and temporary tax relief protected peasants against the vicissitudes of nature, sometimes to great effect, as under Hoshina Masayuki.[5] Still, every increase in the land tax was by necessity a unilateral action not subject to nego-

4. Fields destroyed by floods and other natural disasters were usually treated differently from abandoned fields *(teamarichi)*. In the former case, peasants could petition to have the fields struck from the land registers. In the latter case, if there were no household in the village willing to cultivate the land, it was cultivated collectively *(sōsaku)*.

5. See chap. 2, above, section "Daimyo Bad and Good."

tiation within existing institutions. Unless daimyo were prepared to forego such increases, conflict was inevitable.
Refusal to hear petitions and grant sufficient aid confronted
village leaders with critical choices. The headman and assistant
officers appointed by the fief supervised the economic and social
life of the village—everything from apportioning and collecting
taxes to organizing festivals and public works. Smooth functioning of local government depended on their ability to command
the cooperation of the peasants in the village, and therefore they
were selected from the ranks of the oldest and wealthiest residents. Frequently scions of families which had exercised patri-
archal dominion over the locale in the pre-Tokugawa period,
headmen had special obligations as the heads of lineage net-
works. In addition to particular kinship ties, they assumed general responsibility for the well-being of the village, as symbolized
by the role of keeper of the village's tutelary deities.[6]

Nevertheless, the headman and assistant officers were required to be obedient servants of the ruling class and were held
strictly accountable for their own and the village's behavior. Removal from office, fines, imprisonment, and possibly death
awaited the headman who protested too long and loud against
the lord's taxes. High economic status also carried equally conflicting responsibilities. As the wealthiest villagers, they had the
most to give and the most to lose when economic distress
threatened the village community. Often they went to great
lengths to avoid illegal protests. If the crisis appeared to be
short-term and the headman were rich, he might lend or donate rice to peasants unable to pay their taxes that year. In villages where familial patron-client relationships were strong,
the main house helped its branches.[7] But if the cause of crisis
was the long-term increase in the rate of tax extraction rather
than temporary shortfalls, village leaders were forced to go beyond the village in search of solutions. One course of action was

6. Mitsuru Hashimoto, "The Social Background of Peasant Uprisings in
Tokugawa Japan," in *Conflict in Modern Japanese History*, ed. Tetsuo Najita and
J. V. Koschmann (Princeton, N.J., 1982), pp. 145–163.
7. Ibid., pp. 146–149.

TABLE 1. *Principal Types of Peasant Protests, Japan, 1601–1867*

	Direct appeals	Forceful demonstrations	Petitions	Flight	Smashings	Other	Total
1601–1650	33 (16%)	10 (4%)	50 (24%)	50 (24%)	33 (16%)	33 (16%)	209 (100%)
1651–1700	75 (36%)	27 (13%)	40 (19%)	35 (17%)	10 (4%)	24 (11%)	211 (100%)
1701–1750	98 (23%)	99 (23%)	61 (15%)	35 (8%)	49 (12%)	80 (19%)	422 (100%)
1751–1800	101 (15%)	184 (27%)	44 (7%)	36 (5%)	153 (23%)	152 (23%)	670 (100%)
1801–1850	117 (15%)	164 (20%)	68 (8%)	42 (5%)	187 (23%)	236 (29%)	814 (100%)
1851–1867	41 (11%)	71 (19%)	42 (11%)	8 (2%)	95 (26%)	116 (31%)	373 (100%)

SOURCE: Aoki Kōji, *Hyakushō ikki no nenjiteki kenkyū* (Tokyo, 1966), pp. 36–37.

to defy rules of precedence governing the petitioning process and take the appeal directly to ranking officials. Such protests were called *jikiso* (direct appeals) and *daihyō osso* (direct representations). They became the dominant form of peasant protest relatively early in the Tokugawa period (see table 1).

The Minamiyama Direct-Appeal Movement

Minamiyama was a 54,000-*koku* fief located in the mountainous southwestern quadrant of Fukushima.[8] Only a fraction of the land surface was arable, and the 254 villages were clustered in narrow valleys that veined the rugged mountains. The district belonged to the Tokugawa house, but perhaps because it was poor, inaccessible, and of little strategic importance, during most of the seventeenth century the Bakufu entrusted its administration to the daimyo of neighboring Aizu fief. Under the rule of the Katō daimyo the peasants experienced great hardship and many fled the district; later they enjoyed the benefits of Hoshina Masayuki's fiscal and administrative reforms protective of the livings of small proprietors. During this period (1643–1688), which peasants remembered as no less than a golden age, both population and cultivated land area increased.

The Bakufu resumed direct rule of Minamiyama in 1688. Peasants soon found reason to regret the change in status, for the new administration reversed the previous policy of storing tax rice in local granaries and ordered a thousand *koku* of rice to be shipped annually to Edo.[9] Exporting tax rice was a common practice in most domains, whether ruled by daimyo or the Bakufu, but it caused particular hardship in Minamiyama because the terrain and climate severely restricted rice production. Paddy land was scarce, double cropping was impossible, and only optimum weather allowed peasants to grow enough

8. *Tōhoku shohan hyakushō ikki no kenkyū: Shiryō shūsei,* ed. Shōji Kichinosuke (Tokyo, 1969), pp. 7–8 (hereafter cited as *Tōhoku ikki*).
9. Yamaguchi Kōhei, "Aizu Minamiyama okurairi nōmin sōdō no shuin tara kaimai ni tsuite no kenkyū," *Aizu shi dankai* 31 (1956): 21.

grain to feed themselves and pay taxes. Due to the unstable climate, crop failure was not infrequent, and Masayuki had early instituted a policy of keeping most of the rice in the district and lending it to needy villages. The Bakufu's decision to export tax rice deprived peasants of this much-needed buffer. In 1692 and 1695 drought visited the district. Local reserves proved inadequate, and peasants suffered severe food shortages for the first time in half a century.[10]

The Bakufu returned Minamiyama to Aizu in 1705, only to reverse itself eight years later and resume direct rule of the district. It again ordered peasants to ship tax rice to Edo, and sold nearly half of the grain stockpiled in the interim. Not surprisingly, peasants soon began to protest. At first, villages petitioned individually; but when the Bakufu's intendant ignored the appeals, they organized a broad-based movement. Early in 1714, more than two hundred and seventy headmen and assistant headmen banded together to petition. They argued that unlike farmers in more favorably situated districts, where double and even triple cropping was practiced, they could barely feed themselves:

> From mid-autumn until late in the spring the ground is blanketed with snow, and for half the year it is impossible to do any farming. . . . Many people cannot grow enough food, and every three or four years untimely frosts and storms ruin our crops.[11]

Because of the terrain and climate, peasants in Minamiyama had special needs. In the petition they reminded the Bakufu that Hoshina Masayuki "set aside half the rice as aid for impoverished farmers and provided low-interest loans. This was how we managed to survive." They asked for a return to the former policies, which, they insisted, would allow them to "continue as farmers."[12]

The Bakufu refused to hear the appeal. It continued the shipments of tax rice, and, to make matters worse, began rais-

---

10. *Aizu-Wakamatsu shi*, vol. 4 (Aizu-Wakamatsu, 1966), p. 8.
11. *Fukushima-ken shi*, vol. 10, pt. 2 (Fukushima, 1968), p. 1174.
12. Ibid., pp. 1174–1175.

ing the land tax. Under Aizu's trusteeship the standard tax rate was 48 percent and the tax rate on reclaimed land was 33 percent. Beginning in 1713 the Bakufu raised both categories one or two percent each year, and by 1718 they had risen to 58 percent and 44 percent, representing net increases of 21 percent and 33 percent, respectively.[13] At the same time, it added taxes on millet, beans, and other secondary crops which had not previously been taxed. The peasants were not pleased.

Opposition to the Bakufu's tax policies created special problems for the chief headmen (*gōgashira*), whose role in fief administration was that of intermediary between the intendant acting on behalf of the Bakufu and headmen representing the interests of villages. They were not samurai, but they were the largest landholders and the descendants of rustic warriors who had virtually ruled the district prior to national unification in the late sixteenth century. In recognition of their great influence, the government employed them as supervisors of the nineteen departments which formed the administrative structure of the district. Though not legally members of the ruling class, they were responsible for reporting on the condition of the harvest, recommending reductions in the case of crop failure, administering aid and authorizing loans, as well as organizing and managing public works. The position was hereditary and they received stipends, status privileges, and perquisites which set them apart from headmen and common peasants.[14]

13. *Aizu-Wakamatsu shi*, vol. 4, p. 8.
14. The Bakufu had abolished the chief headman (*ōjōya*) system in 1712, or just before it resumed jurisdiction over Minamiyama. The chief headmen (called *gōgashira* in Aizu) petitioned the Bakufu to be allowed to remain, and the petition was granted. There was opposition to the continuation of the system, however, from some of the village headmen. They in turn petitioned the Bakufu in 1713 asking for the abolition of the system but were refused. It is not entirely clear why the Bakufu made an exception in the case of Minamiyama, but apparently it felt that because of the remote location and widely scattered population, administration would be difficult without the *gōgashira*. The Bakufu employed only one intendant *(daikan)*, while Aizu employed three. It also reversed the policy of paying the stipends (about seven *koku*) of the *gōgashira*, which the peasants now had to pay.

Chief headmen were servants to the warrior class and the nominal representatives of the people, and inevitably the Bakufu's fiscal policies created tension between them and the peasants. In particular, petitions originating at the village level needed their support to ensure a favorable hearing by the intendant. Unless they lobbied strongly on behalf of the appeal, the intendant was not likely to recommend it to his superiors. The efficacy of the appeal process therefore depended to a great extent on the role played by the chief headmen.

Although cognizant of the ambiguous status of these men, peasants expected their support when it was most needed. At first, the chief headmen tried to oppose the resumption of Bakufu rule. In 1712, they jointly petitioned the Bakufu to allow the district to remain a trust territory of Aizu, and to impress the government with the seriousness of the appeal, five of the signers carried the petition to the capital and presented it directly to a Bakufu elder.[15] But when the Bakufu proceeded according to its original plan and appointed a new intendant, most of the chief headmen were not willing to jeopardize their privileged status by persisting in pressing the peasants' growing list of grievances. Despite increasing resistance from the peasants, they cooperated with the intendant in carrying out the unpopular new policies.

Anger at the chief headmen reached new heights in 1718 because of changes in tax assessment and collection to which the peasants objected strenuously. Under Aizu, villages which had unusually small amounts of paddy land had been allowed to commute the entire land tax. In the spring of 1718, however, the intendant ordered that all villages adhere to the general rule which required payment of half the tax in kind. In addition to high costs of baling and transporting, peasants objected vehemently to the threat that this increased dependence on the market entailed. Too poor to stockpile when prices were low, they would suffer but never profit from the volatility of market prices. Nevertheless, the chief headmen consented to the new ruling

15. There is no extant copy of the petition, but its contents are summarized in a subsequent petition. See *Tōhoku ikki*, pp. 186–188.

without prior consultations. Some of the chiefs were engaged in the wholesale grain trade, and perhaps had venal motives. In the direct appeal to the Bakufu written two years later, peasants warned: "If [chief headmen] agree to a matter of such great importance without obtaining our assent, soon there won't be even one peasant farmer to cultivate the lord's fields."[16]

Later in 1718, orders to conduct new surveys of reclaimed land added fuel to the fire. Reclaimed fields were rated lower than older fields, partly to encourage reclamation and partly as compensation for the enormous investment of labor needed to construct new paddy. As part of the effort to increase the land tax, the intendant instructed the chief headmen to reassess the productivity of reclaimed fields; and, on the basis of the surveys, the ratings were made commensurate to the ratings of older fields.[17] Again they carried out the order over the strong protests of the peasants, which again demonstrated where their allegiances lay.

Grievances against taxes and the chief headmen were closely intertwined, and it is not surprising that the peasants raised both issues in subsequent protests. The first action was a demonstration at the intendant's office, in the town of Tajima, late in 1720. On 11/26 (lunar calendar) a crowd of several hundred marched to Tajima with a petition containing five demands— reduction of the tax rate, lower taxes on beans and secondary crops, commutation of the entire land tax, halting of rice exports, and abolition of the office of chief headman. They threatened to stay until the intendant accepted the petition. He refused to receive it, however, and called in the chief headmen, who eventually persuaded the crowd to disband. Without reporting the incident to officials in Edo, he attempted to restore order by arresting the leaders. On information supplied by the chief headmen, two peasants were jailed and four were placed under house arrest.

During the next fortnight, peasant indignation reached un-

16. *Aizu nōmin ikki: shiryō shūsei*, vol. 1, ed. Tashiro Shigeo (Aizu-Wakamatsu, 1978), p. 148 (hereafter cited as *Aizu ikki*).

17. Ibid., p. 148.

precedented heights. There were wild rumors of plans to attack the intendant's entourage if he attempted to return to Edo, and excited groups went daily to Tajima to voice loud complaints. Meanwhile, the real leaders assembled a select group of supporters who met on 12/5 and nominated a well-to-do peasant named Kishirō to lead a delegation of fifteen in a direct appeal to Bakufu leaders. Twenty stayed in Minamiyama to raise funds and rally support for the men who would present the appeal in Edo.[18]

The success of the movement hinged on maintaining an extraordinarily high level of commitment to a course of action which might very well fail and which, whether it succeeded or not, entailed great personal risk. Anticipating the trials that lay ahead, all the delegation swore an oath in writing. They pledged to devote themselves entirely to prosecuting the appeal, to foreswear private interests and frivolous pursuits, to avoid altercations and personal disagreements, and, barring illness, to stay until the matter was brought to a successful conclusion. Anyone whose courage might fail was warned that soon there would be no turning back. It was a grave offense to appeal directly to Bakufu leaders. In fact, the opening words of the oath prophesied the tragedy that lay ahead: "Because the present direct appeal violates the shogun's law, we cannot expect to return alive."[19]

Later they drew up a formal list of grievances. The thirteen-article petition included the complaints about taxes contained in the earlier petition delivered at Tajima and, in addition, accused the chief headmen of embezzling relief funds, underreporting tax receipts, and falsifying financial records. It also claimed that the present difficulties were due to the chief headmen: "Because of the chief headmen, the mercy of the lord does not reach to the peasant, and the appeals of the peasants are not heard by the lord."[20] The petitioners undoubtedly knew that the matter was not nearly so simple, but by putting

18. Ibid., pp. 113–114.
19. Ibid., p. 114.
20. Ibid., pp. 149–150.

the blame on the chief headmen they legitimated appeal to higher authority.

The delegation headed by Kishirō arrived in Edo on 1/22 of the new year, 1721. At first their appeal proceeded smoothly. Descending unannounced upon the pavilion of the Magistrate of Temples and Shrines, they persuaded the officer on duty to accept a copy of the petition. A few days later they did the same at the residence of the Magistrate of Rural Affairs. The petitions were forwarded to Sakamoto Shinzaemon, an executive officer under the Magistrate of Finance, whose office had jurisdiction in suits involving Bakufu intendants. After reviewing the appeal, Sakamoto informed the peasants that the six articles protesting taxes were out of order and could not be heard. He promised, however, to investigate the charge of embezzlement and malfeasance directed against the chief headmen. That inquiry started on 3/3. The chief headmen were summoned to Edo for questioning, and investigations of the headmen followed. By the summer Sakamoto had called in more than two hundred and thirty headmen as well as each of the eighteen chief headmen.[21]

The Bakufu's strategy was to refuse to consider protests against its fiscal policies and hope that the protracted investigation would exhaust the peasants financially, forcing them to stop the protest. The appeal was enormously costly. The peasants had to pay the travel expenses and the food and lodgings of village officials summoned to Edo, and because the inquest began in the early spring and lasted through the summer, even had to cultivate their fields. A few wealthy peasants donated large sums; to pay for the remainder of the expense, villages supporting the protest had to use subscriptions, which, like the land tax, were apportioned according to the size of holdings.[22]

By the summer the cumulative cost of the appeal began to approach the land tax itself, and the leaders found it difficult to raise funds. Moreover, Sakamoto moved the inquest to Tajima

21. Yamaguchi (n. 9 above), pp. 23–25.
22. Muroi Yashiro, "Minamiyama okurairi sōdō oboegaki," *Fukushima shigaku kenkyū fukkan* 9 (1969): 30–31.

in order to interrogate local supporters and completely stop the flow of funds to Edo. Arrests followed and money ran short, but the peasants did not reduce their demands. On 8/22 they drew up a new petition which contained all of the former complaints and even added some new ones, making it clear that they could not compromise on the issue of taxes. After submitting the petition, ten of the peasants headed by Kishirō left Edo secretly and returned to Minamiyama with the intention of organizing a tax strike.[23] The arrest and jailing of Kishirō and several of his confederates undoubtedly blunted the effectiveness of the boycott. Nevertheless, in the autumn the Bakufu received reports of peasants withholding taxes and of villages refusing to reimburse headmen for official expenses if they had sided with the government.[24]

From the beginning the Bakufu had insisted that taxes and administration were not negotiable, and when the peasants' protests went beyond direct appeals, it acted quickly to crush the movement. Twenty officers were sent to Tajima, and Aizu and other fiefs were ordered to send more men. By the early fall, a force of some three hundred officers and soldiers had gathered. They arrested all the known leaders of the protest and launched an exhaustive inquiry to root out sympathizers and accomplices. Beginning on 9/25 every male in the district between the ages of fifteen and sixty was called to Tajima and questioned. When the investigations concluded on 11/28, more than ten thousand peasants had been interrogated and three hundred and fifty jailed or placed under house arrest.[25] More investigations followed in the spring. Finally, the inquest was closed and sentences were handed down. Kishirō and five other leaders were executed; their heads were placed on display outside the prison at Tajima. Forty-three peasants were convicted on lesser charges and punished through land confiscations and fines. Nine members of the group of petitioners died while in prison—an improbable mortality rate.[26] And as for the chief

23. Yamaguchi, p. 40.
24. *Aizu ikki*, pp. 274–275.
25. Yamaguchi, p. 40.
26. *Aizu ikki*, pp. 356, 367–368.

headmen, one was removed from office and five were given warnings.

A month after the executions, when all opposition had been crushed, the Bakufu returned the district to Aizu. Under Aizu the tax rate was not lowered, but aid was more forthcoming. The new administration halted export of tax rice and allowed peasants to commute taxes according to the old formula. The chief headmen stayed in office, but officials increasingly bypassed them in local administration. Their influence declined to the point that they ceased to be the focus of controversy.[27] In defeat, the peasants achieved a measure of success.

Direct-Appeal Movements:
Possibilities and Expectations

Direct-appeal movements, which had occurred as early as 1594, were the dominant form of protest in the middle of the seventeenth century. Between 1650 and 1720, they accounted for 35 percent of all protests against seigneurial authority—double the number of the next largest group. Their predominance, however, did not last. In the early eighteenth century, peasants changed tactics and, in addition to suasion, began to use overt force. Leadership and organization also changed, and by the end of the century peasants rarely made direct appeals except in cases of malfeasance by headmen and local officials. In these circumstances, such appeals to higher authority were necessary, and rulers permitted them.[28]

In spite of their subsequent decline, direct appeals are the best starting point for an analysis of the ideology of Tokugawa peasant movements because they reveal the possibilities and limits of peasants' resistance to seigneurial authority. They show how peasants sought to protect their interests by appealing to norms which the ruling class felt obliged to uphold, and

27. Ibid., p. 370.
28. As early as 1603 provision was made for appeals to higher authority in the event of malfeasance by local officials: Fukaya Katsumi, *Hyakushō ikki no rekishiteki kōzō* (Tokyo, 1979), p. 187–188.

they created precedents for accepted, if unlawful, political action which peasants used to great advantage.

In the early Tokugawa period peasants relied on suasion rather than force. In the Minamiyama movement the peasants assumed that they had legitimate grievances and that the Bakufu would make concessions if they protested long enough. Their first action was to submit lawful petitions. When these failed, they confronted the leaders of the Bakufu directly with their demands. Making direct appeals violated laws which clearly prescribed the appropriate form and content of lawful appeals. Leaders of unlawful protests expected punishment, and because they persisted, knowing the likely consequences, we must conclude that they believed they could obtain satisfaction—that the Bakufu was obliged to render justice above the law. Irwin Scheiner has aptly captured this aspect of direct-appeal movements:

> Peasants believed and acted *as if* they lived in a world of justice, where they were ensured a hearing of their demands by a lord who owed them his benevolence because of his commitment to a higher justice (*gi*) and to the Shogun; and peasants believed they were owed such a justice.[29]

As one would expect, justice did not mean equity, fairness, or evenhanded treatment, since such a conception of class relations was antithetical to the very premises of the proclaimed social order. It does not appear that peasants were asking for impartial administration of laws, either: their actions were illegal and they knew that laws were their enemy. The "justice" that peasants claimed, and lords rendered grudgingly, was defined in terms of normative class roles appropriate to the Tokugawa political economy. They could not expect to receive a "fair" share of the wealth they produced, but they could demand the means to "continue as farmers." Such was the case in Minamiyama. After resuming direct rule in 1712, the Bakufu

29. "Benevolent Lords and Honorable Peasants," in *Japanese Thought in the Tokugawa Period, 1600–1868,* ed. by Tetsuo Najita and Irwin Scheiner (Chicago, 1968), p. 50. Emphasis in source.

had raised *kokudaka* ratings, increased the tax rate, added new categories of taxable products, and resumed shipments of rice to Edo. According to the peasants' petition, tax increases threatened more than half of the landholders with imminent disaster.[30] Probably this was an exaggeration, and, of course, such claims could not be verified until after the damage had been done. In this pass, the peasants used the ideal of seigneurial benevolence to criticize the actual government. Specifically, they claimed that the Bakufu's taxes were higher than those of Katō Akinari, in whose time

> each year taxes increased; tax collection was severe and no mercy was shown to peasants. Since they could not continue as farmers, many abandoned their fields and homes and fled to neighboring domains.[31]

Abandoned rice fields and deserted villages attested to the failure of public virtue. Happily, history had also shown that benevolence would restore the vitality of the countryside and the prosperity of the fief.

> In the twentieth year of Kan'ei [1643], the late Lord Hoshina was enfoeffed and the *okurairichi* [Minamiyama] was entrusted to his administration. Peasants were afforded the same treatment (as the peasants in Aizu). Hearing this, the many people who had fled returned. They were given loans of rice and even farm tools and were able to bring fallow fields back into cultivation. Newly reclaimed land was made totally exempt from taxes or given fifty percent reductions. Now able to preserve their homes and fields and keep their livings in perpetuity, the farmers felt great gratitude toward the ruler.[32]

Peasants could insist on the rightness of their protest because their appeals for lower taxes promised to benefit the lord of the domain no less than his subjects. By drawing on practical

30. Tax collection rose from 21,506 *koku* to 29,248 *koku*, or 36 percent, between 1693 and 1718; from 26,318 *koku* to 29,248 *koku*, or 11 percent, between 1715 and 1718. *Fukushima-ken shi*, vol. 2 (Fukushima, 1971), p. 334.

31. *Tōhoku ikki*, p. 187.

32. Ibid.

lessons of statecraft, they proposed a formula for resolving conflict based on complementary class roles rather than competing interests. They also eschewed violence and accepted punishment, thereby acknowledging both the power and the authority of titular rulers. How could such appeals be refused? In fact, as in the Minamiyama movement, most direct appeals were settled by harsh punishment of the leaders *and* the granting of at least some of the peasants' demands.

The peasants' reliance on suasion reflected the power relationship between lord and peasant in the early Tokugawa period. Before the separation of warriors and farmers and the disarming of the peasant class, villages and leagues of countrymen had taken up arms and fought to defend local interests. The number of armed uprisings declined steadily after Hideyoshi's reforms and the establishment of the Tokugawa hegemony. In many areas, however, local control was comparatively incomplete and, in the first half of the seventeenth century, peasants were more likely to flee from oppressive taxes than appeal directly to the lord.[33] By the mid-seventeenth century— the end of the reign of the third shogun, Tokugawa Iemitsu— the essential political, legal, and ideological institutions of seigneurial rule had been firmly established, and it is at this point that peasants turned overwhelmingly to direct appeals. Having abandoned rebellion and flight, they used their status as peasants legally bound to farm specific plots of land to justify political protest, arguing that the lord was obliged to protect small proprietors against default.[34] Though the costs were very great, most direct-appeal movements succeeded in obtaining "justice" above the law: lords reduced or canceled taxes; the

33. Between 1590 and 1649 there were 53 *chōsan* movements (21 percent of all movements) and 34 direct appeals (14 percent). The number of direct appeals increased dramatically in the latter half of the century, 75 cases (35 percent), while the number of *chōsan* movements declined equally dramatically, 35 cases (16 percent). Aoki Kōji, *Hyakushō ikki no nenjiteki kenkyū* (Tokyo, 1966), pp. 36–37.

34. Fukaya, *Hyakushō ikki*, p. 66.

leaders of the protest accepted martyrdom. As long as both played their respective roles, direct appeals provided a mechanism for resolving conflict over the land tax.

Demonstrating in Force

Not all protests in the early Tokugawa period were as peaceful and respectful of authority as direct appeals. Sometimes unruly crowds marched on the lord's castle town and refused to disband until promised satisfaction. The first protest of this kind in the Fukushima area occurred in Naganuma, a small fief of 16,000 *koku* situated in southern Fukushima, in response to the tax policies of the daimyo Matsudaira Yoritaka.[35] Enfeoffed in 1700, Yoritaka did not increase the land tax, but he taxed cotton spinning and cash crops that peasants depended on to supplement farm income. He also ordered peasants to transport tax rice to his warehouse in Edo.

It is likely that the peasants petitioned against the taxes and that the appeals were denied, though the records leave the point in doubt. We know that instead of organizing a direct appeal, the farmers demonstrated in force. In the spring of 1702, Genjū and Toemon, small proprietors described as being on the verge of losing their land, published a circular (*kaijō*) calling for a mass meeting. Sympathizers carried the circular from village to village, and a few days later a large crowd gathered at a field not far from the fief administrative office. Led by Genjū and Toemon, they marched on the office and refused to disperse until the ranking officer accepted a petition asking for repeal of the new taxes. Afterward Lord Yoritaka granted tax reductions, but he also arrested Genjū and Toemon, who were paraded from village to village in shackles and executed on the very spot where the crowd had assembled for the march.

The details of the demonstration (*gōso*) reveal some of the

35. *Tōhoku ikki*, p. 566.

differences between these movements and direct appeals. They were popular movements that mobilized non-elite peasants; the leaders were likely to be small proprietors, rather than headmen; and, by using a measure of force, they went one step beyond direct appeals in challenging seigneurial authority.

Examination of a large and well-documented uprising that occurred in Aizu in 1749 affords a better understanding of such movements.[36] Late in the summer of 1749, wind and freezing rain caused severe damage to crops of villages located in the foothills of Mount Bandai and around the shores of Lake Inawashiro. For five years farmers in this part of Aizu fief had been plagued by bad weather, and after this disaster to the harvest they desperately needed aid.[37]

At first the fief promised loans of rice and seed, for without assistance many would lose their land. The matter appeared to have been settled when a new clique of officials headed by magistrates Saigō Niemon and Namigawa Tasaku came to power and pushed for a tougher policy.[38] They insisted that villages accepting loans repay the full amount, even though it was customary to discount at least part of the debt to compensate peasants for their losses. Further, villages were to agree in advance not to ask for additional concessions: they would not be allowed to delay or reschedule tax payments or apply for exemptions on uncultivated fields. And as a final measure, Saigō and Namigawa reduced the loans to a third of what had first been promised.[39]

The protest began in Eboshigoya village, where the peasants decided that because of the new terms the promised aid would prove insufficient. The village headman cautioned against making illegal protests, but the majority of the peasants were prepared to take direct action. Joined by neighboring villagers, they gathered a large crowd and marched on the district office at Inawashiro-chō. The intendant refused to listen to their complaints, berating the crowd for disorderly behavior and in-

36. Ibid., pp. 40–75, 152–176.
37. Ibid., p. 41.
38. Ibid.
39. Ibid., p. 42.

sisting that if they had legitimate grievances they were obliged to submit written appeals. Upon hearing this, they reportedly shouted that petitioning was fruitless and, denouncing the absence of reliable officials, announced their intention to march on the castle town.[40]

As the peasants began the march on Aizu-Wakamatsu, the fief's castle town, they became increasingly aggressive. In one incident a group encountered an inspector who had come to supervise the distribution of loans, which they now refused to accept. Inspectors were high-ranking officers who normally commanded fear if not respect. But when the inspector tried to caution the crowd, he was met with jeers. One peasant flew into a rage and, shouting that the inspector was an ass, rushed at him and knocked him down.[41]

As the crowd marched toward Aizu-Wakamatsu, small groups fanned out to raise recruits. In many villages they succeeded, but not if the headman steadfastly opposed the demonstration. We know, for example, that in Matsuzaki and Nishidate villages the headmen challenged the emissaries. They warned against joining illegal protests and threatened to inform against anyone who joined, arguing that since their villages were comparatively well off and did not need aid, there was no reason to participate. The emissaries claimed that even so the villagers must come because the protest was "for everyone." Making no progress, they threatened to bring the crowd to "set fires and slaughter everyone." But neither pleas nor threats had much effect in villages where the headmen used the full weight of their authority to oppose the protest. The emissaries who had come to rally support departed alone.[42]

Although support for the demonstration varied from village to village, the march continued to gain momentum. Several thousand peasants gathered at Shiokawa, a village situated a short distance north of Aizu-Wakamatsu, and there the leaders stopped to draw up a list of grievances. The document they

40. Ibid., pp. 44–45.
41. Ibid., p. 47.
42. Ibid., p. 58.

produced contained numerous complaints arranged under seven headings. Taxes were much too high, and the constant addition of new taxes and cancellation of old taxes was very confusing. The fief demanded too many reports from headmen, wasting time and money; and frequent inspection tours by high-ranking officials imposed added burdens, since villages were obliged to provide food and entertainment and often bribes. The greater part of the petition, however, criticized apparent indifference to the peasants' plight:

> For the last five years we have suffered crop failure, and in mountain villages many fields lie fallow. For five years this has continued, and we are barely able to keep living as peasants. But although we petitioned frequently, not one in ten of our appeals was heard.[43]

Leaving Shiokawa, the crowd marched on Aizu-Wakamatsu, where officials, anticipating their movement, had barricaded roads leading into the castle town. The crowd, undeterred, set up camp, singing, chanting, and throwing stones over the outer walls. At one point, some peasants tried to storm the palisades blocking access to the inner city. Rumors that they had broken through led fief officials to flee with their families for refuge behind the secure walls of Aizu castle. Then a detachment of riflemen rushed to the gate and fired a single volley, which sent the attackers fleeing.[44] This was the only clash. The crowd was unarmed and had come to win concessions, not to sack the city. But they refused to disperse.

The fief soon decided to conciliate the crowd. The only alternative was to use force, which was ample, but such tactics might only trigger even greater disorder. In this situation, clique rivalry proved to be decisive in determining the official response. Magistrates Saigō and Namigawa had come to power three months earlier as part of a clique of officials who advocated aggressive fiscal measures to reduce the fief's debt. The leaders of the opposing clique, magistrates Yamazaki San'emon and Ariga Daifu, seized the opportunity presented by the up-

43. Ibid., p. 41.
44. Ibid., p. 49.

rising to denounce their rivals and take power by citing the need to return to policies of benevolent rule.[45]

Back in command, Yamazaki and Ariga acted quickly to pacify the crowd. They ordered wealthy townsmen to distribute food, drink, and firewood to the peasants, and the next day rode boldly through the city gates to announce that Saigō and Namigawa had been dismissed and that the government was now prepared to give a careful hearing to all grievances. They repeatedly urged the crowd to return to their villages. The peasants cheered the news of Saigō's and Namigawa's fall, but refused to disperse. They demanded temporary tax reductions, in addition to loans, and protested that dismissal was too light a punishment for officials as tyrannical as Saigō and Namigawa, who, they reportedly cried, should be brought back to the countryside and made to do the work of peasants.[46]

Two days later, the government decided that additional concessions were needed to put an end to the protest. Once again the magistrates rode out into the crowd. This time they promised tax reductions. Having been betrayed only a few months earlier in the negotiations for the loans, the peasants demanded proof that the promises would be honored, and Yamazaki and Ariga agreed to issue a formal proclamation.

Aizu officials kept promises made to the crowd and ordered tax reductions of up to fifty percent to villages that had suffered the greatest losses and somewhat smaller reductions where damage had not been as severe. The proclamation that announced the reductions did not refer to the demonstration or the power struggle among the councillors of the daimyo. It simply stated that taxes had been reduced in order that peasants could "adequately feed their families and continue for many years as farmers."[47] Now dominated by the "benevolent rule" faction, the government was prepared to acknowledge the legitimacy of the peasants' complaints and take steps to alleviate their plight. Benevolent rule, however, did not exclude harsh

45. *Aizu-Wakamatsu shi,* vol. 4, p. 25.
46. *Tōhoku ikki,* p. 48.
47. Ibid., p. 52.

measures to discourage future protests. Aizu soldiers went from village to village, arresting hundreds of suspected participants, who were interrogated and tortured. Six months later, eleven persons believed to have been the leaders of the demonstration were executed and two hundred and eighty received lesser punishments.[48]

Protests in the Mid-Tokugawa Period

The ruling class was deeply concerned by the forceful protests and took various countermeasures. Most prominent was legislation ordering harsh penalties. The Bakufu code promulgated in 1742 stipulated that the leaders of violent demonstrations were to be executed, the headmen of participating villages expelled from office, assistant officials' lands confiscated, and the whole village fined in proportion to its *kokudaka*.[49] In the Aizu uprising, the leaders were executed and participants were fined; yet despite severe punishments the number of demonstrations increased. Hoping to persuade peasants that such protests would not succeed, the Bakufu published an edict in 1769 stating that if peasants conspired and formed a great crowd, "even if the appeal ought to be granted it shall not be accepted no matter what its merits."[50] It also adopted laws designed to strengthen the military capabilities of daimyo in quelling disturbances. An edict issued in 1769 permitted fief authorities to dispatch troops to neighboring domains in the event of uprisings, and authorized the use of firearms, which had previously been forbidden.[51] A more subtle strategy was to pay public homage to the leaders of direct-appeal movements, hoping that the peasants might choose to emulate the peaceful protestations and respectful demeanor of martyred heroes of the seventeenth century. On a more practical level, the govern-

48. Ibid., p. 54.
49. Yasumaro Yoshio, *Nihon no kindaika to minshū shisō* (Tokyo, 1974), p. 151.
50. Ibid., p. 150.
51. Hayashi, *Hyakushō ikki no dentō* (n. 2 above), p. 24.

ment made an effort to facilitate lawful petitions against corrupt and high-handed district officials who were the cause of many violent demonstrations.

Bakufu and daimyo had reason to be disturbed. Although they were not faced with armed uprisings, peasants had begun to demonstrate in force and to evince greater consciousness of power relationships and possibilities for exploiting weaknesses inherent in the structure of local control.[52] The military power of the warrior class was unchallengeable, but there were practical limits to its use in compelling compliance. Daimyo ruled from castle towns and could not actively police every village. Peasants' observance of fief laws and payment of taxes depended on their willingness to do what was expected. Thus, when peasants descended on the lord's castle town and refused to disperse, they signaled the temporary end of cooperation. It was up to the daimyo to restore an acceptable relationship.

Despite the change in the form of collective action, the ideology of protest had not changed. As in direct appeals, peasants asked for limited concessions which they justified in terms of protecting the livings of small proprietors. In their appeals they attributed their troubles to evil officials who had only temporarily and illegitimately gained control of the government. As in the Aizu uprising, the peasants' passionate denunciation of magistrates Saigō and Namigawa went hand-in-hand with acceptance of legitimate authority.[53] Once the virtuous officials proclaimed the return to benevolence, the rebellious crowd dispersed. Demonstrations rarely lasted more than three or four days, and peasants even appear to have accepted the inevitability of punishment. They were not penitent, as some leaders of direct-appeal movements were reported to have been. They tried to avoid detection: for example, the circulars and manifestos were anonymous documents which concealed the village of origin. But after the uprising, peasants who had played prominent roles and were likely to be identified and apprehended did not flee the domain. Only rarely did the crowd

52. Fukaya, *Hyakushō ikki* (n. 28 above), p. 50.
53. Yasumaro, *Kindaika shisō*, p. 185.

make amnesty a condition of disbanding. They often demanded written proof of the promises made,[54] but did not dispute the lord's right to execute leaders of illegal demonstrations, even when the demonstrations were acknowledged to be for just cause. The demonstrations were costly gambits carried out within the framework of political and economic relationships premised on the hegemony of the warrior class and the legitimacy of its rule. They were not rebellions.

If analyzed solely from the point of view of peasant-lord relations, the movements appear to be little more than direct appeals which used a measure of force to frighten the ruling class into granting concessions. But such an analysis misses the real significance of eighteenth-century peasant protest—the dramatic entry of non-elite peasants as the principal actors in rural conflict.[55] With very few exceptions, the leaders of direct appeals were men of high social and economic status. Three of the six leaders of the Minamiyama movement were headmen and two were assistants. Moreover, the leading participants— the thirty who signed the compact—came from the village headman class.[56] Kishirō, the charismatic leader and apparent mastermind of the protest, did not hold office, but his was an old family that had settled the village and was said to have descent from noble warriors.[57] It was the attribution of distinguished ancestry rather than its authenticity that was significant in the direct-appeal protests, reminding us of the normative relationship between high status and leadership in peasant society.

Sometimes headmen led large demonstrations, but in more cases than not they joined reluctantly, urging caution at every step, tagging along at the onset and disappearing as soon as possible.[58] They had every reason to hang back. Punishment of

54. Ibid., p. 185.
55. Fukaya, "Hyakushō ikki" (n. 3 above), p. 114.
56. Muroi (n. 22 above), p. 30.
57. *Tōhoku ikki*, p. 194.
58. Yasumaro Yoshio, "Minshū hōki no sekai zō," *Shisō*, 586 (April 1973): 545–546.

headmen who instigated demonstrations was especially severe, but if they stifled the protest they were eligible for rewards.[59] Rather than headmen, the leaders of forceful demonstrations tended to be small proprietors who feared becoming "broken farmers." They could not wait indefinitely upon the lord's justice, and low status and little formal education made them less susceptible than the elite peasants to Confucian teachings that taught respect for hierarchy and obedience to authority.[60] Lacking the same material and psychological restraints, once convinced of the need for action they were more inclined toward violence.

In the eighteenth century as in the seventeenth, the village provided the structure for mobilization; collective action, however, no longer followed formal lines of hierarchy. The decision to act was made not by the headman but by the *sōbyakushō*— village landholders acting as a body. In most cases the question of participation was debated at a meeting attended by all householders. Low-status peasants might take the lead in arguing for the protest and high-status against, but once a consensus was reached everyone was expected to join. The men who had argued in favor became the actual leaders, regardless of their economic status, and anyone who refused to join or attempted to subvert the movement could become the target of sanctions— fines, destruction of property, even ostracism.[61] Just as unanimous participation was required of the villagers, peasants from neighboring villages were expected to join. A few days in advance, leaders circulated a secret notice; once under way, the crowd marched through the district to compel compliance. As in the Aizu uprising, villages that held back were threatened with reprisals. In a similar protest that occurred in the Shindatsu area of Fukushima a few days earlier, the leaders published a circular warning: "Any village that obstructs or refuses to lend a hand is the enemy of all the people"; because such

59. Yasumaro, *Kindaika shisō*, p. 220.

60. Fukaya Katsumi, "Bakuhansei ni okeru muraukesei no tokushitsu to nōmin tōsō," *Rekishigaku kenkyū: Bessatsu tokushū* (November 1972): 112.

61. Yasumaro, *Kindaika shisō*, p. 217.

actions "injured all the people," the circular declared, "homes will be set afire and everyone slaughtered."[62]

Whether direct appeals or demonstrations, the movements reveal a high capacity to mobilize peasants living in the same jurisdiction. In large part, the peasants' ability to organize is explained by the absence of supervision and policing by agents of the ruling class. After the removal of samurai retainers to castle towns, villages enjoyed considerable freedom to manage their affairs. Headmen of villages in the same administrative subdivisions often met to discuss directives sent from the castle, and managed public works projects such as irrigation, roads and bridges, and flood control. Being actively involved in administration, they had practical experience in working together, as well as in defending parochial village interests. They could just as easily meet to draw up a petition as to apportion corvée labor needed to dam a river. Moreover, villages in the same fief were linked by a courier network. Normally used to disseminate edicts and proclamations, the network was used by peasants to communicate with other villages as part of political mobilization. Of course, the degree of unity actually achieved varied considerably. Unity of purpose and sustained mobilization were greatest when headmen organized and directed the movements, as in the Minamiyama direct appeal. Successful mobilization in mass demonstrations often required maintaining secrecy until the last possible moment, since unsympathetic headmen might inform the authorities, thereby nipping the movement in the bud. The leaders of these movements understood that extraordinary measures and emotional appeals were needed to overcome voices of caution and peasants' justified fears of the inevitable mass arrests and executions that followed illegal protests. Yet the violent language of the circular cited above should not be read literally. The threats were hyperbolic. Peasants sometimes destroyed the property of headmen and pawnbrokers, but they never burned down whole villages, nor were people killed. Instead, the threats and

62. *Tōhoku ikki*, p. 87.

the language of the circulars revealed a radical, antihierarchical element in these movements. The language is instructive: the key term used was *banmin* (all people), a phrase rarely used in petitions;[63] in petitions peasants identified themselves as *onbyakushō* ("honorable peasants"), which denoted a status in the feudal polity.[64] One also sees instances of boasting and aggressive posturing. In the Aizu uprising peasants acted boldly, transcending everyday constraints on behavior; they jeered at, insulted, and even attacked officials. As noted earlier, one inspector was thrown to the ground. In another incident, a frightened intendant ran from his lodgings dressed only in bedclothes and chose to spend the night hiding on a snow-covered mountain rather than face the aroused mob.[65] This was not warfare, but peasants did harass officials before whom they would normally have bowed respectfully.

Mobilization in forceful protests occurred outside the village political and social hierarchy and empowered the peasants to make extraordinary demands on the rich, who might be forced to entertain the crowd with food and drink, cancel debts and return pawned goods, and join in illegal demonstrations. The understood purpose of the mass mobilizations—protection of peasants' general rather than individual interests—allowed peasant crowds legitimately to make extraordinary demands of elite peasants, just as they had made them of the daimyo. An incident from the 1749 Aizu uprising illustrates the peasants' logic: The day after the fief acceded to peasants' demands for tax reductions, a poor farmer went to the home of a pawnbroker in Shiokawa to ask for the return of farm tools and seed which he had pawned earlier that year in a final effort to keep his land.[66] He had nothing left but his land and the unharvested winter crop, and no money to redeem his tools and seed, but he pleaded with the pawnbroker to return his goods, at least until after the autumn harvest. Because the fief had re-

63. Ibid.
64. Fukaya, *Hyakushō ikki*, pp. 65–68.
65. *Tōhoku ikki*, p. 60.
66. Ibid., pp. 58–59.

duced taxes, he argued, he would surely be able to repay the debt in full by the end of the year. To this the pawnbroker was reported to have replied that it would be a simple matter if he were the only one, but all the other clients would demand the same favor, ruining his business. Angered by this reply, the peasant persuaded others in debt to the pawnbroker to appeal together. Still, the pawnbroker refused to return goods until paid in full. His meanness proved to be his undoing. The peasants, feeling that they were collectively threatened by his refusal, flew into a rage and attacked his house. They were soon joined by other peasants who in a furious rampage destroyed his property.

Another result of these mass mobilizations was that the peasants who came together in large numbers experienced feelings of power. In 1738, for example, in the fief of Taira, central Fukushima, peasants who were demonstrating against increased taxes surrounded the castle town and reportedly threatened to reduce the fief to "black earth."[67] In this and other cases the sense of potency did not last. The hope of receiving "benevolence" ceded ultimate power in the situation to the authorities. As long as obtaining benevolence remained their goal, their apparent power was certain to be fleeting.[68]

One sees in the forceful demonstrations of the eighteenth century new aspects to peasant collective action which involved representation, mobilization, and tactics. There are two sets of circumstances which account for the rise of the new movements: the fiscal needs of the seigneurial class, and changes in social relations at the village level.

At the end of the seventeenth century, the Bakufu and daimyo encountered real financial difficulties for the first time and, in response, initiated reforms designed to cut expenses

67. Ibid., p. 718; Fukaya Katsumi, "Bakuhansei shakai no kaikyū tōsōshi kenkyū ni tsuite," *Rekishi hyōron* 289 (May 1974): 22–35, makes the important point that statements such as this one should not be read literally, since the authors of chronicles of peasant uprisings tended to exaggerate and romanticize peasants' behavior, particularly their bravery and daring.

68. Yasumaro, *Kindaika shisō,* pp. 168–169.

and raise tax revenues. These policies provoked stiff resistance, since the early growth in population and reclaimed rice fields, which had allowed lords to increase tax revenues without necessarily appropriating a larger percentage of the surplus, ended in the seventeenth century. Without the expansion of primary agriculture to support the political economy of institutionalized benevolence, daimyo faced much harder choices when confronted with appeals for emergency aid and tax relief. As the cost of receiving peasants' petitions rose, the seigneurial class naturally tended to be less willing to acknowledge the legitimacy of their complaints. A change in the tactics of mobilization became necessary to achieve comparable effect.

The breaking down of the traditional relationship within the village between hierarchy and political representation was the second factor. Two trends should be noted. On the one hand, village headmen did not generally lead or support forceful demonstrations, and they might even become the object of attack if they obstructed mobilization. On the other hand, middle- and low-status peasants not only joined in discussions but also organized the movements and articulated collective demands. Did the headman's reluctance to lead these demonstrations force common peasants to take the initiative, or did upstarts preempt the headman's role? Accounts of forceful demonstrations provide ample evidence that both occurred to some degree, and conceptually it is not necessary to establish a cause-and-effect relationship since the changes in role behavior were part of a dynamic process of social change involving peasants of high and low status. Beginning in the seventeenth century with the registration of small peasants as proprietors, formerly dependent families linked to high-status households through familial patron-client relations became increasingly independent. Economically, they were less likely to exchange labor services for land and material assistance; socially, to observe the ritual roles associated with membership in the patron's family lineage. The attenuation of functioning patron-client relationships, which had organized peasants' social and economic life during the earlier period, undermined the traditional relationship between hierarchy and leadership. High-status peasants, the traditional spokesmen for the village, felt less compelled to represent the collectivity; and small proprietors, deprived of the social insurance that the former relationships had provided, urgently demanded seigneurial benevolence.

It is important to remember that the goals and ideology of collective action did not change to any great extent. The confiscatory system of land rents and the village's liability for payments still compelled a certain type of collective political action. Because of the need to maintain a favorable balance between village land and population, as fiscal pressures on the horizontally incorporated community reached impossible levels, peasants of every status became acutely aware of their vulnerability as individuals. Thus, in protest movements, the village united, villages joined other villages, and headmen and the heads of the leading families were expected to forcefully represent peasants' grievances to the ruling class. Collective action continued to offer the only real hope for mitigation of hardship, even though changes in the rural economy led to a breakdown in the traditional relationship between hierarchy and leadership. Depending on the particular circumstances, middle- and low-status peasants assumed responsibility for mobilizing the community.

4. New Causes of Conflict

In the latter half of the Tokugawa period, increased production for the market created new conflicts between lord and peasant. How and why peasants began to produce for the market and the effect of rural commodity production on economic growth are questions which need not detain us, for they are adequately addressed in English-language scholarship and the next chapter will look carefully into the development of sericulture and the effects on village social structure.[1] Hence only a brief sketch is presented below.

Peasant commodity production began in the latter part of the seventeenth century in the broad, fertile Kinai plain surrounding Kyoto and Osaka in response to consumer demand from rapidly growing urban populations. Osaka was the "storehouse" of Japan, and its merchants collected agricultural products and raw materials from the countryside and shipped food and manufactured goods to Edo. In the first phase peasants with good access to the Osaka market employed technologies— land reclamation, double cropping, high-protein fertilizers, la-

1. Thomas C. Smith, *Agrarian Origins of Modern Japan* (Stanford, Calif., 1974) and "Farm Family By-Employments," *Journal of Economic History* 29 (December 1969): 687–715; Susan Hanley and Kozo Yamamura, *Economic Growth and Demographic Change in Preindustrial Japan, 1600–1868* (Princeton, N.J., 1977).

bor-saving inventions—which increased the output of traditional crops. To the extent that productivity exceeded tax quotas, they were able to market the surplus and diversify production, which led to a second phase of development as certain villages and regions specialized in producing cash crops. Cotton was the most important crop, followed by rape seed, vegetable dyes, sugar, and tobacco. The third phase was characterized by the proliferation of agricultural by-employments and small-scale manufacturing: sericulture, cotton spinning and weaving, and charcoal, wax, and paper making. At each stage greater participation in the market had the effect of breaking down the traditional extended family and large-farm households comprised of kin and non-kin dependents; increasingly, small landholders established themselves as economically independent peasant farmers. Cooperative labor also declined.

The same changes did not occur in all villages, nor at the same time throughout the country. On the whole the Kinai and Inland Sea regions in western Japan developed early, eastern and northeastern Japan later.[2] Within each region topography, natural resources, and administrative controls greatly affected development, producing variants of the general pattern. In some "early developing" villages, growing rice was so profitable that cereals continued to dominate the peasant economy; in "late developing" Shindatsu in Fukushima, the climate and soil were well-suited to sericulture, and raw silk and silkworm-egg cards supplanted traditional farm products. Because some daimyo established and strictly enforced monopolies on local products and collected produce as part of the land tax, agricultural specialization did not always lead to greater peasant participation in the market. Occasionally, rural manufacturing developed even though agricultural productivity lagged. In Morioka, for example, the climate and tax structure limited agricultural growth, but resources favored iron manufacturing.[3] Nevertheless, despite differences in timing and degree, a common trend is clearly discernible; during the latter half of the

2. Hanley and Yamamura, pp. 19–28.
3. Ibid., pp. 131–137.

TABLE 2. *Peasant Protests, Japan, 1601 – 1867*

	Number	Average number per year
1601 – 1650	209	4.2
1651 – 1700	211	4.2
1701 – 1750	422	8.4
1751 – 1800	670	13.4
1801 – 1850	814	16.3
1851 – 1867	374	22

SOURCE: Aoki Kōji, *Hyakushō ikki no nenjiteki kenkyū* (Tokyo, 1966), pp. 36– 37.

Tokugawa period higher productivity, cultivation of cash crops, by-employments, and manufacturing greatly increased peasants' participation in the market.

The frequency of peasants' protests in the latter half of the period suggests that, whatever the effect of commodity production on overall farm output, peasants became more disputatious as participation in the market increased. See table 2. Aoki Kōji's data show that the average number of protests rose particularly sharply after 1750, when, by most estimates, commodity production spread beyond the early developing districts of western Japan. Moreover, it is unlikely that the greater frequency of protest was due to the same condition which had sparked peasant resistance in the seventeenth century, the rigorous use of cadastral surveys to maximize the *kokudaka* land tax. Although the data on tax collection are far from complete, they show that collection of tax rice reached a peak in the first half of the eighteenth century, leveled off in the second half, and declined thereafter.[4] In part the decline can be attributed to peasants' demands to commute a larger portion of the land tax—a phenomenon to be discussed presently. For example,

4. Yamazaki Ryūzō, "Edo kōki ni okeru nōson keizai no hatten to nōminsō no bunkai," *Iwanami kōza Nihon rekishi*, vol. 12 (Tokyo, 1963), pp. 342– 343; Thomas C. Smith, "The Land Tax in the Tokugawa Period," in *Studies in the Institutional History of Early Modern Japan*, ed. John W. Hall and Marius B. Jansen (Princeton, N.J., 1968), p. 294.

Bakufu records show that commuted payments rose from 30 percent in the early eighteenth century to 45 percent in the mid-nineteenth century. But it should also be noted that in addition to greater commutation, total revenue from the land tax failed to grow after 1730–1740.

The data presented above suggest a correlation between peasant participation in the market and increased conflict, but the relationship between the two is far from certain. The relationship becomes clearer, however, if one compares data on peasant movements in Aizu, where commodity production developed late, with data from Shindatsu, where sericulture developed rapidly from the middle of the eighteenth century.

Various factors retarded commodity production in Aizu *han* and the neighboring Bakufu trust territory of Minamiyama.[5] Rugged mountains surrounded Aizu and Minamiyama and the absence of waterways and turnpikes made transportation slow and costly, thus limiting peasants' participation in markets beyond the fief. Moreover, Aizu's rulers did not permit free trade; instead, they established monopolies on the principal cash crops—lacquer, ginseng, and wax. In order to protect the tax base, they made repeated efforts to prevent the sale of land and to limit the interest that could be charged on pawned land. In most areas the seigneurial class tried to prevent market relationships from undermining the traditional economy, but in the late eighteenth century Aizu officials actually ordered wealthy peasants to return to the original owners land that had been acquired by debt foreclosure.[6]

Aizu was also well administered. A single daimyo house— the descendants of Hoshina Masayuki—ruled Aizu and took pride in maintaining feudal traditions and firm control of the domain. The enduring strength of traditional warrior loyalties within the fief was demonstrated at the end of the Tokugawa

5. Shōji Kichinosuke, "Shōhin seisan no hatten to kisei jinushisei no seiritsu," *Shōgaku ronshū* 23, no. 5 (1955): 148–149.
6. Shōji Kichinosuke, "Aizu han ni okeru tochi bunkyūsei," *Rekishigaku kenkyū* 103 (September 1953): 19–20.

period, when Aizu samurai fiercely resisted the overthrow of the Tokugawa Bakufu.

Mountainous, isolated, tightly ruled, and economically backward, Aizu and Minamiyama contrasted at every point with the Shindatsu district. Shindatsu contained a broad river valley, and its location assured good communication to the north and south. The Oū Kaidō, one of the five turnpikes linking Edo to the provinces, ran the length of Shindatsu and was used by merchants and daimyo traveling between Edo and the northeastern provinces. The retinue of the daimyo of a fief as large as Sendai included three hundred retainers, who would stay, during their leisurely journeys, for three days at major stations on the road. There were stations at Koori, a market town, and at Fukushima, a castle town. The provisioning of food, lodging, stables, and miscellaneous services to travelers stimulated economic development, as did the growth of the commercial carrying trade.[7] In addition to the good communications, and of greater ultimate importance, was the rapid development of sericulture in the eighteenth century, and its dominance of the regional economy thereafter.

Feudal control in Shindatsu was weak, for the district included more than ten separate jurisdictions, most of which were too small to support a regular corps of resident officials, and although the Bakufu maintained intendants at Koori and Kawamata, the offices were understaffed. Only Fukushima *han*, a fief with an assessed productivity of 30,000 *koku*, had a large samurai population. Most fiefs in Shindatsu were detached fiefs (*tobichi*) and trust territories (*azukechi*) administered from distant castle towns; some were merely villages assigned to high Bakufu officials as income supplements.

Owing to the fragmented nature of feudal rule, administration was slack, and it was impossible to enforce strict control over commodity production and trade. Rulers did tax peasants' production; for example, the Bakufu levied a tax on braziers used to steam cocoons in preparation for reeling raw silk, and

7. *Fukushima-ken shi*, vol. 3 (Fukushima, 1970), pp. 1017–1018.

TABLE 3. *Regional Data on Peasant Protests, Fukushima,*
1600–1867

Region	1600–1699	1700–1799	1800–1867
	(Total number and average per decade)		
Fukushima (all areas)	26 / 2.6	57 / 5.7	67 / 10
Aizu / Minamiaizu (western Fukushima)	13 / 1.3	13 / 1.3	8 / 1.2
Shindatsu (north central Fukushima)	0 / 0	18 / 1.8	26 / 3.8

SOURCE: *Tōhoku shohan hyakushō ikki no kenkyū: Shiryō shūsei,* ed. Shōji Kichinosuke (Tokyo, 1969), pp. 28–34.

in the late eighteenth century taxed villages that specialized in the manufacture of silkworm egg cards. But the taxes were relatively light—less than two percent of the value of the egg cards—and did not hinder development.[8]

Data on peasant movements in Aizu and Shindatsu show very different trends in the latter half of the Tokugawa period. See table 3. In Aizu, where the peasant economy changed less, the number of movements remained constant, while in Shindatsu the number increased dramatically, beginning in the eighteenth century. Why protests increased in Shindatsu is indicated by data on the principal causes of peasant protests and uprisings. See table 4. To show more clearly the factors that contributed to the rising number of protests, I have distinguished between protests against higher taxes and protests against collection of taxes in kind.[9] Between the eighteenth and nineteenth centuries, protests against tax increases disappeared while those against collection of tax rice increased ten-

8. Araki Moriaki, "Yōsangyō no tenkai to Tokugawa ki no jinushisei kosaku kankei," in *Yōsangyō no hattatsu to kisei jinushisei,* ed. Furushima Toshio and Takahashi Kōhachirō (Tokyo, 1958), p. 136.

9. Conflict over collection of taxes in kind involved two issues: opposition to the shipment of local rice paid as taxes to Edo (*kaimai*), and demands that a portion of the land tax be commuted to cash payments at a rate below the market price (*yasukokudai*).

TABLE 4. *Principal Causes of Peasant Protests,*
Shindatsu District, 1700–1867

Cause	1700–1799	1800–1867
	(Number and percentage in each period)	
Tax increases and cadastral surveys	5 (28%)	—
Payment of taxes in kind	1 (6%)	10 (36%)
Aid and relief	7 (38%)	7 (25%)
Headman malfeasance	2 (11%)	6 (21%)
Other	3 (17%)	5 (18%)
Totals	18 (100%)	28 (100%)

SOURCE: *Tōhoku shohan hyakushō ikki no kenkyū: Shiryō shūsei,* ed.
Shōji Kichinosuke (Tokyo, 1969), pp. 28–34.

fold and those against headmen showed a threefold increase.
How can these trends be explained, and what light do they shed
on conflict in the late Tokugawa period?

Collection of Taxes in Kind

In 1858 the headmen of six villages in northern Shindatsu petitioned the Bakufu asking that they be allowed to commute the
portion of the land tax heretofore paid in rice. In the petition
they also raised objections to shipping tax rice (*kaimai*) to Edo
instead of storing it locally.

The villages that petitioned had previously been under the
jurisdiction of a small private fief which had permitted peasants
to commute most of their taxes into cash payments, and the rice
collected as taxes had been stored in granaries in nearby market
towns, readily available in the event of crop failure. In
1857 the Bakufu assumed direct control of the villages and ordered that the peasants pay half of the land tax in kind and

transport the rice to Edo. Speaking on behalf of their villages, the headmen protested: "It has now been ordered that tax rice must be sent to Edo. We are unaccustomed to this procedure, and it is causing us considerable expense. Moreover, since last year, severe drought has reduced the harvest, and we are hard pressed to find enough rice to keep us alive."[10]

The headmen went on to remind the Bakufu that the peasants in their villages earned their living chiefly from sericulture, and that, as a consequence, incomes varied considerably, depending on how much silk they harvested. "Everybody was counting on a successful silk crop to make it through the year. But because of unseasonable weather in the spring, many of us are now destitute."[11] They asked the Bakufu to suspend shipments of tax rice to Edo; and, as a further concession, asked that the cash rate for commuted taxes be set in the autumn, when peak supplies depressed the market price.

Two years later the headmen of Nagakura, Okabe, Koori, and seven other villages petitioned the Bakufu for permission to commute the entire land tax. These villages being major producers of raw silk and silkworm egg cards, the headmen described how sericulture affected the village economy:

> In this district, the principal economic activity is mulberry husbandry and silkworm rearing. The silk we produce is purchased by people who come from other provinces, and the cash earned pays our taxes and allows us to purchase daily necessities.[12]

These and other sericulture villages in Shindatsu did not grow enough rice.

> Each year a great number of migrant workers come to this area to find work during the silkworm rearing season. They, too, must be fed, and because most of the land in our villages is unirrigated, even in normal years there isn't enough rice to go around. Consequently, we purchase much rice from other provinces.[13]

10. *Tōhoku shohan hyakushō ikki no kenkyū: Shiryō shūsei*, ed. Shōji Kichinosuke (Tokyo, 1969), pp. 374; hereafter cited as *Tōhoku ikki*.
11. Ibid.
12. Ibid., p. 376.
13. Ibid.

The headmen explained that the present predicament had been caused by successive years of crop failure locally and in neighboring domains that normally sold rice to Shindatsu, causing shortages and high prices. "Prices have risen steeply, and since local rice production is not enough to feed us for even half the year, we are now in a desperate situation."[14] They closed the petition by asking that payments of taxes in rice be commuted to cash payments and that the commutation rate be fixed to protect against sudden price increases.

The petitions reveal how peasants' dependence on purchased rice due to participation in the market made them resistant to paying taxes in kind. In economically advanced rural areas, the consumption of rice often exceeded the local supply, and in northern Shindatsu, where sericulture was most highly developed, only thirty percent of the arable land was irrigated paddy field suitable for growing rice.[15] In some villages where dry land had been converted to mulberry cultivation to provide feed for silkworms it was as low as nine percent.[16]

Specialization in sericulture was a rational response, given the resource endowment of these villages, but it was not without dangers. Crop failure occurred frequently in northeastern Japan, causing short supply and high prices made worse by the collection of taxes in kind. Because rice was needed both for consumption and for taxes, demand tended to be inelastic and any shortage immediately affected prices. It is not surprising, therefore, that Shindatsu had a higher proportion of movements against the payment of the land tax in rice (36 percent) than areas outside of Shindatsu (10 percent).

Revolt against the Village Headman

Table 4 also shows that complaints of wrongdoing by village headmen made up a sizable number of the protests recorded in

14. Ibid.
15. Shōji Kichinosuke, *Meiji ishin no keizai kōzō* (Tokyo, 1954), p. 149.
16. Araki, "Yōsangyō," p. 113.

Shindatsu and were particularly numerous in the nineteenth century. One illuminating revolt against the village headman occurred in 1859 at Moniwa, a village in northwestern Shindatsu under the jurisdiction of the Bakufu intendancy at Koori. The village contained some two hundred households totaling about a thousand people and divided into two wards. Located in a deep valley on the Mogami River and surrounded by thickly wooded mountains, it had relatively little arable land; the average holding was under five *koku*, or less than was needed for subsistence from agriculture alone. Most peasants raised silkworms and manufactured charcoal; these by-employments sustained the village economy.[17]

The headman of Moniwa village, Sashichi, had inherited the office from his father. In 1859, the combined tenure of father and son had lasted more than forty years.[18] The immediate cause of the revolt was peasant suspicion that Sashichi had embezzled public funds. Several years earlier, peasants in a neighboring village had brought suit against their headman for misuse of famine-relief funds, and disclosures made during that investigation prompted peasants in Moniwa to scrutinize Sashichi's disposition of similar funds. The evidence they uncovered moved them to request an official investigation, but the Bakufu intendant, Fukuda Shōzaemon, repeatedly refused their requests. Not receiving satisfaction at the district level, they next petitioned directly to the office of the Finance Magistrate in Edo.[19]

By going over the head of the intendant, the peasants forced him to take up their complaint. It is not clear whether Fukuda received orders from Edo, or whether after learning of the petition he acted in anticipation of instructions from his superiors; but shortly after the petitioners returned from Edo he summoned Sashichi and the plaintiffs to an inquest at Koori. There, Sashichi at first denied any wrongdoing. Under persistent questioning from his accusers, however, he admitted to certain "errors" in his management of village funds. Realizing that

17. *Fukushima-shi shi*, vol. 9 (Fukushima, 1971), pp. 125–131.
18. *Tōhoku ikki*, p. 403.
19. Ibid.

the admission was a strategic error, he immediately complained that he felt ill. Over the strong protests of the peasants, Fukuda suspended the inquest. Instead of handing down a verdict, he appointed a local notable to act as mediator with responsibility for negotiating a settlement.[20]

During the next two weeks the mediator worked out a tentative settlement whereby Sashichi would resign and the plaintiffs drop the charges of embezzlement. It seemed to be acceptable to both parties, but at the last moment Sashichi changed his mind, broke off the negotiations, and went into hiding. Fukuda, the intendant, had left Koori by this time, having been rotated to a new post, and the new intendant had not yet arrived. During the interim Yamaguchi Shinosuke, a Bakufu officer on circuit tour, came to Koori and was soon approached by the plaintiffs. Yamaguchi ordered both sides to appear at the intendancy, and scolding the peasants as well as Sashichi, instructed them to adhere to the terms of the initial settlement. But after Yamaguchi departed Sashichi reneged on an important part of the settlement by refusing to return tax records and other documents relating to the village's finances, which rightfully belonged to the new headman. The peasants appealed to the former mediator and the new intendant, both of whom declined to enter the case. The plaintiffs then approached Sashichi's relatives, who agreed that he should release the documents. Eleven representatives went to Sashichi's house and accused him of duplicity and bad faith. A heated argument ensued, at the height of which Sashichi grabbed the key to the storehouse and his sword, and bolted from the house, wounding one person before mounting his horse and riding off, but also dropping the key. Opening the door of the storehouse, the peasants saw thousands of items of personal property—furniture, clothing, valuables—which over the years villagers had pawned and lost. Fearing arrest if they repossessed them directly, they carried the goods to the local temple for safekeeping.

The Bakufu intendant, who had previously refused to repri-

20. Ibid.

mand Sashichi, now acted with great zeal to punish the peasants. He sent twenty soldiers to the village who from morning
to night roughly interrogated the residents, not omitting some
women and children. A hundred and forty peasants were arrested and marched off to Koori. Most were released after a
few days, but eighteen who were considered the leaders of the
anti-Sashichi movement were held in jail.

Despite the arrests, the peasants continued to agitate and
sent emissaries to neighboring villages to complain about the
handling of the dispute. Soon after, the intendant appointed
three headmen from villages in Shindatsu to investigate, but
picked friends of Sashichi who reported in his favor. Despairing
of receiving justice locally, the peasants once again organized a
direct appeal to Edo, addressed this time to a high-ranking Bakufu official, Matsuyama, from Sendai *han*.[21]

We do not know why Matsuyama took up the peasants'
cause. Perhaps he feared that any prolonging of the dispute
would lead to more violence, and since Moniwa bordered on
Sendai, unrest could spread to his domain. On the other hand,
he may have acted simply to render justice. In either case, his
intervention brought about a quick settlement when he ordered the release of the peasants incarcerated at Koori.
Sashichi thereupon realized that he had been outflanked and
agreed to a settlement—one far more costly than the earlier
agreement he had broken. In addition to resigning and surren-
dering the documents, he paid 800 *ryō* as compensation for
funds that he and his father had embezzled during their long
tenure as headmen, returned several plots of land acquired ille-
gally, and canceled all outstanding debts owed by peasants in
the village.[22]

The revolt against Sashichi provides insights into local conflicts and the twists and turns of seigneurial justice. Embezzlement, tax manipulations, and other abuses of financial power
were frequently the cause of movements against headmen,

21. Ibid., p. 404.
22. Ibid., p. 410.

since they apportioned and collected all taxes of their villages—powers which dishonest headmen abused. In Moniwa, for example, several decades before the revolt just discussed, the Bakufu had ordered a general increase in the land tax. Sashichi exempted his own very large holdings and saddled the peasants with the new charges. He also paid only a small portion of the tax assessed on braziers used in processing raw silk.[23]

During the dispute the local intendant, Fukuda Shōzaemon, consistently supported Sashichi. As we have seen, Fukuda first refused to investigate the peasants' charges; when finally forced to hold an inquest, he allowed Sashichi to leave at an opportune moment. Later, when Sashichi broke the agreement, the new intendant tolerated his violations, but when the peasants unlocked Sashichi's storehouse, he immediately sent troops into the village. The leaders were imprisoned, and Sashichi was returned to the village, apparently triumphant.

Sashichi's influence, however, did not extend to the higher levels of the Bakufu bureaucracy, so the villagers were able to obtain justice through direct appeals to Edo. The favorable treatment of Sashichi by the intendant is explained by the weakness of local administration in territories such as Shindatsu where Bakufu intendants were appointed for short terms after which they were rotated to new posts. The permanent staff at Koori included only eight officers and some foot soldiers, though they administered many widely scattered villages. Thus, they depended on the cooperation of the headmen and were reluctant to take actions which might alienate them. Officials in Edo had different priorities. Their chief concern was to prevent local disputes from becoming violent movements. In their desire to maintain political order, they were not disposed to protect individual headmen.

The successful prosecution of the campaign against Sashichi was possible because his ill-gained wealth and his arrogance had alienated the entire village, not just the poorest peasants. The average holding in Moniwa was only 3.5 *koku*, while

23. Ibid., p. 408.

Sashichi's were ten times as large.[24] He was wont to ride his horse through the cultivated fields, and he forced peasants to work on his private holdings. Fifty-seven villagers signed the initial petition calling for an inquest, and when Sashichi continued to behave in an arrogant fashion as the dispute developed, the village united in its efforts to bring him down. The plaintiffs included the headman of the lower ward and two assistant headmen. Thus, the group aligned against Sashichi included people with sufficient wealth and status to make their complaints heard beyond Shindatsu. Twice they had to appeal to Edo. Appeals often took weeks, and the direct and indirect costs were considerable. It took two years, but they managed to oust Sashichi.

Economic Conflict in the Village

The protest against Sashichi was more than a revolt against a corrupt and unpopular headman. In addition to being the headman, Sashichi was the largest landowner, and there is reason to believe that his activities as landlord and moneylender to peasants in the village created antagonisms that contributed to the intensity of the peasants' opposition.

In the petition to Matsuyama, the peasants claimed that "the common people of the village all borrowed money from Sashichi, who increased his wealth while they lost what little they had." The result of this unequal economic power was made dramatically clear to the peasants who broke into Sashichi's storehouse: "The collection of pawned goods . . . so filled the room that it was impossible to step inside." The petition continued: "During the more than forty years that Sashichi and his father served as headmen, they used the authority of their office to dispossess the common people."[25] Sashichi most flagrantly and profitably abused his power by treating a village

24. *Fukushima-shi shi,* vol. 8, (Fukushima, 1968), pp. 487–527, contains land and population data on Moniwa village in 1866.
25. *Tōhoku ikki,* pp. 403–404.

fund originally established to provide aid to the poor as his private property. He lent this money at usurious interest rates and used it as capital for financial ventures outside the village, especially for the buying and selling of raw silk. He also refused to permit sake wholesalers to enter the village, which forced the peasants to purchase the rice wine he brewed.

It is easy to imagine how the activities of wealthy peasants as usurers and landlords created tensions and antagonisms in rural society. Even if they adhered scrupulously to the terms of the contract, their demands for payment of rents and interest frequently caused strife, especially when crop failure made it difficult for the peasants to meet their obligations. Moreover, as implied by the accusations against Sashichi, wealthy peasants sometimes used high status to unfair advantage in their dealings with other peasants. In the case of Sashichi we have only the charge, but the incident described below shows how a poor peasant's land might be expropriated by elite peasants. The principal actors were Yoshino Shutarō, a wealthy landlord and silk merchant; Shōzaemon, head of Shutarō's branch household, residing in a neighboring village; and Kichirōji, a poor peasant from Shutarō's village.[26]

The incident began in 1863 when Kichirōji borrowed money from Shutarō. Kichirōji pledged his land as security for the loan, and agreed to repay the entire sum with interest by the last day of the year. Shutarō assumed that Kichirōji would default and, even before the expiration date had passed, gave the land to Shōzaemon, the head of his branch household.

Contrary to Shutarō's expectations, Kichirōji returned several weeks before the deadline to repay the loan. Shutarō explained that Shōzaemon now had the documents pertaining to the loan, and advised Kichirōji to discuss the matter with Shōzaemon. But when Kichirōji went to Shōzaemon's house, he was informed that the land still belonged to Shutarō, and that he would therefore have to return to Shutarō's house.

When Kichirōji reappeared to ask for the return of his land, Shutarō made various excuses and told him to be patient. Dur-

26. Shōji Kichinosuke, *Yonaoshi ikki no kenkyū* (Tokyo, 1970), p. 227.

ing the next two weeks Kichirōji twice tried to repay the loan and repossess his land. Each time, Shutarō and Shōzaemon put him off. Kichirōji waited until after the New Year before again visiting Shutarō. This time he was informed that the deadline had passed and that he had therefore defaulted on the loan. Kichirōji, incensed, went to complain to the village headman. The headman listened to his story but told him, "It would be most difficult for a person like you to bring suit against men such as Shutarō and Shōzaemon." He warned Kichirōji that litigation was a very costly affair, more than a poor man like Kichirōji would be able to afford. He strongly advised Kichirōji to abandon his efforts to reclaim the land. The headman consulted with other village officials and all agreed that the dispute should be settled by informal agreement. To Kichirōji they promised to work out an arrangement whereby he would become Shōzaemon's tenant on his former land. They emphasized that this arrangement "would spare everybody in the village a great deal of trouble," and they hinted that if Kichirōji refused their good offices, he could expect no further help.[27] Having little alternative, Kichirōji consented to pay Shōzaemon an annual rent of seven *hyō* (sacks) of rice.

Kichirōji's troubles were not over. The following year Shōzaemon increased the rent by 2 *hyō*, despite the fact that unfavorable weather had reduced the harvest. Kichirōji tried to persuade Shōzaemon to put off the rent increase until the next year, but Shōzaemon refused and threatened to evict him unless he signed a new contract with the higher rent.

Kichirōji signed the contract, but being nearly destitute he was forced to use his entire rice harvest to feed his family. When Shōzaemon discovered this, he told Kichirōji that unless he paid the entire sum by the end of the year, he would be replaced by another tenant. Kichirōji appealed to his relatives for help, and although they were very poor, they contributed one *hyō* of rice. Kichirōji took the rice to Shōzaemon as a down payment, promising to pay the rest after the next harvest. Shō-

27. Ibid.

zaemon refused to accept anything less than the full rent, and repeated his threat to evict Kichirōji.

We do not know the outcome of the dispute. The document which contained the events summarized above was a petition written by the assistant village headman to the local government office. The petition asked fief officials to instruct the headman to order Shōzaemon to accept the one *hyō* of rice as a down payment. The petition also stated that they, the village officials, had agreed to guarantee Shōzaemon the full rent should Kichirōji be unable to pay after the next harvest.[28]

We can only speculate as to how Kichirōji fared subsequently. Perhaps the officer acted on the petition and ordered Shōzaemon to take the down payment, and in the autumn Kichirōji harvested enough rice to pay his debts. By being diligent, frugal, and unimaginably determined he might even have saved enough money to buy land and acquire a measure of security. The scenario is possible but not likely; what is known about subsequent events in Shindatsu suggests that the odds were stacked heavily against him. During the next two years the district suffered crop failure, disruption of trade, and unprecedented inflation. The well-to-do hoarded rice, raised interest rates, and refused credit to peasants who had nothing to pawn. Kichirōji had already pawned and lost his land; he had begged and borrowed from relatives who were little better off than he. It is difficult to imagine that he managed to recover his land.

Kichirōji's fate remains obscure but not that of Yoshino Shutarō. He became the rural entrepreneur par excellence. Starting with a sizable fortune built from usury, landholding, and the manufacture and marketing of silk, he became even richer during the export silk boom that followed the 1859 opening of Yokohama. In 1875 he organized his own trading company, which bought local raw silk and egg cards and sold directly to exporters.[29] Ten years after the Meiji Restoration, when he had surely forgotten all about cheating Kichirōji out of a small piece of land, Shutarō had become the wealthiest man in Shindatsu

28. Ibid.
29. Shōji, *Meiji Keizai*, pp. 308–309.

and his son was a pioneer in finance and industry, helping to establish five regional banks and the Fukushima Power and Light Company.[30]

Individuals as lowly as Kichirōji may lead obscure lives, but there are occasions when their collective anger makes history. One such moment was the great uprising that swept Shindatsu in the late spring of 1866, described in detail in chapter 6. As a postscript to the incident of Kichirōji's lost land, we note that on the morning of the fifth day of the uprising a crowd attacked and destroyed Shutarō's sake brewery and the property of his relatives in the same village.[31] We wonder but will never know how many peasants like Kichirōji were avenged by the act.

The disputes discussed above occurred in the mid-nineteenth century, or more than two hundred years after the first conflict we examined—the flight of two thousand peasants oppressed by daimyo Katō Akinari of Aizu. What changes and continuities are apparent?

Peasant protests in the seventeenth century revealed the profound impact of the *kokudaka* system, which created the need for institutionalized seigneurial "benevolence," and of the separation of warrior and farmer, which disarmed villages and made the seigneurial class absentee landlords. Under these conditions high- and low-status peasants united against the fiscal demands of the ruling class. To be sure, some conflicts set peasants against other peasants: neighboring villages fought over boundaries, mountains, meadows, and water; peasants disputed the headman's financial accounts, apportionment of taxes, and perquisites; new arrivals in the village challenged old residents to gain membership, political representation, and access to communal resources; hereditary and bonded agricultural servants struggled to win from masters a degree of personal and economic freedom. In the first half of the Tokugawa period, however, conflict between the seigneurial and peasant classes was predominant. Most peasants lived in a subsistence

30. *Fukushima-ken shi,* vol. 22 (Fukushima, 1972), p. 525.
31. Shōji, *Yonaoshi ikki,* p. 50.

economy in which all but a fraction of what was not rendered to the lord was consumed or exchanged locally; likewise the seigneurial class controlled the land tax, and the dispensation of loans and tax relief determined whether small peasants "continued as farmers" or were "broken." Thus, there was a strong need to maintain class unity which undoubtedly inhibited the expression of conflict within peasant society.

During the last century of the Tokugawa period the number of peasant movements increased, yet collective action by peasants did not necessarily unite high- and low-status villagers. In areas where market relationships predominated, wealthy peasants took on economic roles as moneylenders, landlords, and merchants which generated social conflict. If, as in the case of Sashichi of Moniwa village, the abuse of high status was blatant and affected the entire community, they were likely to become the targets of collective action by the peasants of their villages. And there were countless cases of the abuse of high status, such as the incident involving Yoshino Shutarō and Kichirōji, which left a legacy of bitterness even when the victims did not strike back.

Despite the increase in social conflict, however, the new economic relationships did not invalidate the old model of collective action. All peasants regardless of their wealth shared an interest in opposing new taxes, petitioning for aid after natural disasters, and protesting payment of taxes in kind. Especially in areas like Shindatsu where rice was frequently in short supply, village headmen no less than the lowly peasant farmer wanted to be able to commute a larger portion of the land tax and to have rice collected as taxes stored locally. As in the early Tokugawa period, headmen still performed the "traditional" role of advocate of the village's collective interests.

5. Sericulture and Village Economy in Shindatsu

At the end of the Tokugawa period the largest and most violent rural protests occurred in areas of eastern Japan where sericulture flourished. What was the connection?

This chapter analyzes sericulture production in the Shindatsu district of Fukushima where, in 1866, tens of thousands of peasants rioted for six days. It was the most destructive peasant movement during more than two and a half centuries of Tokugawa rule, and no larger movement has occurred since. To account for the uprising and assess its significance one must understand the economic and social effects of sericulture on the peasant economy, and this will require analyzing the mode of production.

Development of Silk Production

Sericulture is the rearing of silkworms to produce silk fiber and silkworm egg cards, and includes mulberry husbandry, which supplies the feed consumed by silkworms. To raise silkworms, the producer incubates the eggs and nurtures the larvae until they reach maturity and spin cocoons. If the producer wishes to harvest raw silk, the cocoons are boiled to kill the pupa before the moth breaks through its silvery sheath. Boiling also loosens the fiber in preparation for reeling silk from the sterile cocoons. To manufacture silkworm egg cards, the producer waits until the moths emerge and mate. The sheets of paper matting on which the female moths lay their eggs are collected and stored in a cool place until the next spring, when the cycle begins again.

Silkworms consume enormous quantities of mulberry leaves, and commercial sericulture is only feasible where mulberry trees thrive. Mulberries grow well in sandy soil and require plenty of water. Waste and marginally fertile land near rivers and streams provides an excellent natural environment, and in this respect the geography of the Shindatsu region favored the early development of sericulture.[1] Shindatsu is a river basin bordered by parallel mountain ranges, the Ōu Mountains to the west and north and the Abukuma to the east. The basin is approximately thirty kilometers long and is broader at the southern end than the north. The Abukuma River, which flows through the basin, is the tenth longest in Japan. Its headwaters are in the Nasukazan district of Ibaragi prefecture; it enters Fukushima at the southwest and flows north through the prefecture before emptying into the Pacific Ocean south of Sendai. Fed by 246 tributaries which, in the spring, greatly increase the river flow, it often floods, spreading silt and wash. Frequent flooding, particularly at the northern end of the Shindatsu basin, makes land near the river and along tributaries ill suited for growing rice but excellent for mulberries.[2]

Sericulture began in villages in northern Shindatsu situated close to the river and along tributaries, where the danger of flooding is greatest. It is thought that the first plantings were intended to curtail soil erosion, and that only later did peasants start to raise silkworms for profit. In the early seventeenth century, a daimyo, Uesugi Kagekatsu (1555–1623), actively encour-

1. Yamada Shun, "Shindatsu chihō no sanshugyō," in *Nihon sangyō shi taikei,* vol. 5 (Tokyo, 1960), p. 73.
2. Ibid., p. 75.

aged the industry in an effort to enrich his domain, which had been severely reduced in size by the victorious Tokugawa.[3] By the middle of the seventeenth century, Shindatsu silk producers were selling raw silk to weavers in the Nishijin district of Kyoto and wholesalers in Omi province. Demand increased at the end of the seventeenth century after the government restricted imports of Chinese silk. In the eighteenth century, peasants in the district began producing high-quality silkworm egg cards. By the middle of the century, metropolitan wholesale trading houses had established branches in Shindatsu and contracted with local merchants to buy on consignment. At the end of the eighteenth century, the district was widely recognized as one of the leading producers of raw silk and silkworm egg cards in the country.[4]

During the early Tokugawa period, most silk producers in Shindatsu were wealthy peasants, and the remarkable growth of the industry was due in large part to their efforts to develop new strains of silkworms and mulberries.[5] The quality and amount of silk spun depended on the vitality of the silkworms and their resistance to cold, dampness, and disease. By continually crossbreeding local and imported strains, scientifically minded producers in Shindatsu developed silkworms well adapted to the region's specific environmental conditions. The first advances were made in the seventeenth century, but the middle decades of the eighteenth century were the most dynamic years for innovation. Between 1740 and 1780, five new strains were produced: they were hardier and more likely to survive to maturity; because they grew faster, the rearing cycle was shortened; and they spun thicker and more lustrous thread, which was easier to reel and fetched higher prices.[6]

Successful sericulture also requires that producers have reliable access to enormous quantities of freshly picked mulberry leaves throughout the silkworms' six-week rearing cycle. In the Shindatsu basin, native varieties of mulberries flourished in the

3. Ibid., p. 73.
4. *Fukushima-shi shi*, vol. 2 (Fukushima, 1972), pp. 563–564.
5. Yoshida Isamu, *Satō Tomonobu* (Aizu-Wakamatsu, 1979), pp. 17–18.
6. *Fukushima-shi shi*, vol. 2, p. 559.

lowlands, but did not grow well in dry and hilly land. In the middle of the seventeenth century, however, Shindatsu sericulturists successfully crossed the sturdy and cold-resistant "Yamaguwa" strain with the "Shiraguwa" which required less fertile soil and a warmer climate.[7] The result was a tree which possessed the best qualities of both parents. They also introduced mulberry strains from neighboring provinces which they crossed with local ones. In fact, fourteen of the fifty-two mulberry strains grown in Japan at the end of the Tokugawa period had originated in Shindatsu.[8]

In addition to silkworm breeding and mulberry husbandry, producers in Shindatsu pioneered improved rearing techniques. Because silkworms are very sensitive to cold and humidity, sericulturists normally burned wood and charcoal to heat and dry out the rearing rooms. In the late eighteenth century, producers noticed that if they let the fires burn continually and maintained a constant, high room temperature, the silkworms ate faster and fed for longer periods of time. They also discovered that the length of the cycle depended on feeding; the more the silkworms ate, the sooner they reached full growth and spun cocoons.[9]

The discovery of the effects of temperature on feeding, and of feeding on maturation, had important implications for sericulture as it was practiced in the Tokugawa period. Without heating, the number of days required for silkworms to spin cocoons depended chiefly on the weather. Warm weather stimulated the silkworms' appetites and made them grow rapidly, while cool weather had the opposite effect. For example, records from the eighteenth century show that the cycle ranged from a maximum of fifty-one to as few as thirty-seven days.[10] Burning fires and maintaining a high, even temperature reduced the cycle to less than five weeks and made it more predictable.

Discovered in the late eighteenth century and widely prac-

7. Shōji Kichinosuke, *Kinsei yōsangyō hattatsu shi* (Tokyo, 1964), pp. 56–57.

8. Yoshida, *Satō*, p. 22.

9. Shōji, *Yōsangyō*, pp. 77–78.

10. Ibid., p. 92.

ticed in Shindatsu in the nineteenth century, heating techniques helped small families to integrate sericulture and traditional farm activities by minimizing potential conflict between
labor peaks in silkworm rearing and rice cultivation.[11] During
the last weeks of the silkworms' rearing cycle, small families
needed the full-time labor of every member. By developing an
early-budding mulberry, producers could incubate the eggs in
the latter half of April. But as long as maturation depended on
the weather, varying from five to more than seven weeks, the
final week, which was also the busiest, sometimes occurred in
early June, when rice seedlings were transplanted and farming
required the constant attention of the whole family. Because of
this risk of labor overlap, households able to hire workers were
best qualified to take up silkworm rearing as a commercial enterprise. By shortening the cycle, heating minimized the risk of
overlap; and because of reduced risks, small peasant farmers
increasingly took up sericulture.

Technology and Economy of Scale

Genetic improvements, advances in mulberry cultivation, and
surer techniques in silkworm rearing enhanced productivity
and, by making production more predictable, reduced risk to
some degree. Practices developed in the Tokugawa period did
not, however, allow producers to economize on labor. Because
production could not be mechanized, sericulture remained
highly labor intensive.[12] And, as will be seen, the demands put
on workers minimized potential economies of scale. Poor peasants could produce on a small scale as efficiently as large-scale
sericulturists,[13] largely because of the habits and particular
needs of silkworms.

11. Ibid., p. 72.
12. Yamada, "Shindatsu sanshu," pp. 82–83.
13. Ōishi Kaichirō, "Meiji zenki ni okeru sanshugyō no hatten to jinushisei,"
in *Yōsangyō no hattatsu to kisei jinushisei*, ed. Furushima Toshio and Takahashi
Kōhachirō (Tokyo, 1958), pp. 420–423.

Of all the tasks involved in rearing silkworms, feeding is the most demanding. Silkworms sleep only four times, each time for about twenty-four hours, before spinning cocoons, and if not sleeping they will eat voraciously day and night. As the larva grows from a newly hatched "ant" to full size, it consumes 30,000 times its body weight in mulberry leaves, which must be picked, chopped, and distributed fresh at every feeding. Moreover, it is very particular about what it will eat, choosing only the tenderest portions of the leaf. Experiments have shown that silkworms consume at most 12 percent, and as little as 6 percent, of the prepared leaves.[14] The remainder, which dry out, cannot be used again. Fresh leaves must be prepared, and any effort to economize on the number of leaves will reduce consumption, which in turn slows growth and reduces the quantity and quality of silk spun. Scientific studies have shown that 450 kilograms of leaves are needed to rear the larvae hatched from a standard silkworm egg card.[15] Rearing silkworms for profit is unavoidably labor intensive.

Labor demand is also uneven. The quantity of feed increases daily and reaches enormous proportions at the end of the growth cycle. For example, during the first of the five feeding periods, larvae hatched from one card need two kilograms of leaves, or less than one half of one percent of the total amount they will eventually consume. By the last feeding, they need 340 kilograms, or 75 percent.[16] The number of workers available at labor peaks determines the limits of production, unless the family is able to hire additional labor. According to estimates based on late eighteenth-century records from Fushiguro village, rearing one card required the labor of two workers.[17] Even a large family could not rear more than two cards without employing outside labor to help pick, chop, and distribute the leaves.

14. Yoshimaro Tanaka, *Sericology* (Bombay, 1964), p. 53.
15. Ibid., pp. 46–47.
16. Ibid., p. 63.
17. Sasaki Junnosuke, "Hōreki-Kansei ki ni okeru sanshu keiei," in *Yōsangyō no hattatsu to kisei jinushisei* (n. 13 above), p. 244.

Handbooks on sericulture written during the Tokugawa period gave detailed instructions on the best methods for raising
silkworms. Written by successful sericulturists with a practical
and scientific interest in silkworm rearing, these handbooks repeatedly emphasized the great care that was needed to maximize output. Perhaps typical was the following passage from
the opening pages of the *Yōsan hiroku* ("Confidential record of
silkworm rearing"), written by Kanō Tanboku, a well-to-do
peasant who used the pen name Uegaki Morikuni:

> Everyone, both young and old alike, must be extremely attentive to
> the needs of the silkworm. Think about them constantly and ne-
> glect nothing that has to do with their rearing. Be occupied with
> them utterly day and night, and your care will be rewarded with
> success.[18]

Kanō went to great length to specify areas of particular concern. He stressed, for instance, that the first five to six days after
hatching were critically important. During this period, the
young larvae must be fed eight times a day. The leaves should
be picked and chopped fresh for each feeding, and workers
were cautioned to take great care to see that the feed and the
"ants" were distributed evenly in the rearing trays to ensure ad-
equate feeding in the initial period of growth.[19]

Another handbook gave even more detailed instructions for
the first feeding period. It stated that young silkworms should
only feed on the choicest parts of mulberry leaves, and that
these should be chopped crosswise. Leaves cut too close to the
stem are tough and difficult to digest: "Young worms cannot eat
well and therefore become thin. But if the center part is fed to
them, the worms grow fat and their sleeping and waking will be
regular."[20]

18. Ouekaki Morikouni, *Yo-san-fi-rok*, trans. Johann Joseph Hoffmann
(Paris, 1848), p. 56. My references are to this French edition, as I have been
unable to consult a Japanese edition. Hereafter cited as Kanō.

19. Ibid., p. 82.

20. Quoted in Thomas C. Smith, "Ōkura Nagatsune and the Technologists," in *Personalities in Japanese History*, ed. Albert Craig and Donald Shively
(Berkeley and Los Angeles, 1970), p. 139.

Rearing silkworms for profit thus demanded not only time and energy but also diligence and attentiveness. To relax one's concentration at any point could spell disaster. For instance, in the *Yōsan hiroku* are the following observations:

> Certain stupid persons will become preoccupied and they will suddenly be astonished to discover that it is time for the next feeding. They run in search of leaves, and they tear off the leaves without care or caution. To make up for lost time, they crush the silkworms under a mountain of leaves. When as a result of insufficient care in feeding, the worms at last grow sickly, these people exclaim, "They are dying by themselves!" What a triumph of ignorance.[21]

Feeding demanded the most labor, but was only one of a number of time-consuming and exacting tasks in rearing silkworms. Because they are extremely susceptible to disease, Kanō advised that the rearing trays be cleaned of litter two or three times a day. No less important was careful regulation of the temperature of the rooms. Undue cold, heat, or humidity could prove fatal: "Take the greatest precautions with regard to any change in the interior temperature. It is a principal requirement for successful rearing."[22] Satō Tomonobu, a silk producer from Kakeda village in Shindatsu, wrote in his manual on silkworm rearing that the producer should keep watch through the night. There were no thermometers at the time, and he advised that by carefully observing the movements of sleeping children, one could detect changes in temperature and take appropriate action to protect the silkworms. It was truly a labor that knew no end.[23]

The author of the *Yōsan hiroku* emphasized that silkworms were "frail creatures that demand the most minute ministrations," and he added, by way of encouragement, that in return for hard work and constant attention, "the silkworms will procure most considerable benefits for their keepers."[24] The

21. Kanō, p. 57.
22. Ibid., pp. 63–64.
23. Yoshida, *Satō*, p. 215.
24. Kanō, p. 64.

health of silkworms and the quality of the silk ultimately depended on meticulous execution of a great number of tasks. Carelessness, inattention, or bad judgment at any point in the rearing process could jeopardize the entire enterprise. In his references to silkworm workers, Kanō apparently assumed that most labor would be performed by members of the sericulturist's family, especially women and children. Family members would share the rewards; it was therefore reasonable to expect them to work hard for long hours, and to guarantee success by performing innumerable "minute ministrations."

Agricultural laborers, hired for brief periods, required guidance and supervision. Unlike members of the household, they did not have the same interests or obligations. Their relationship to the keeper was contractual; they were paid by the day and did not share in the profits that accrued from a particularly successful harvest. Little in their situation was likely to make them as motivated as household labor. Scholars have noted that day laborers were not considered sufficiently dependable to work without extensive supervision.[25] The larger and more impersonal the work force, the greater was the need for guidance and discipline. Thus, supervision was the chief hidden cost in large-scale production, and it greatly limited economies of scale.[26]

Advances in the technology of sericulture increased the productivity of labor, but the full potential for higher productivity could be realized only if workers were skilled and highly motivated. This factor favored small-scale production using family labor. Moreover, the fact that technology was cheap and readily available contributed to the growth of small-scale production. Rearing silkworms did not require expensive equipment, since small producers could use part of their house in lieu of specially constructed sheds. The technology, which consisted of improved strains of silkworms and mulberries and better techniques of rearing, was disseminated freely.[27] Thus, there was

25. Yamada, "Shindatsu," p. 88.
26. Ibid.
27. Smith, "Ōkura," pp. 147–149.

little to prevent poor peasants from becoming producers if they had sufficient manpower. Even if they borrowed to finance operating expenses, the entire production process took less than two months, which allowed a quick return on investment.

A further incentive to small production was that family labor was unpaid. As in other agricultural by-employments, sericulture enabled families to increase their income by more fully utilizing existing labor resources, as noted in the following passage from the *Yōsan hiroku:* "Sericulture is the work of women, and it does not sacrifice the labor of men. It is a secondary occupation, but one which is very lucrative, since it utilizes labor not used in farming."[28] Of course, wealthy peasants also used household labor, and their families tended to be larger. But if the scale of production began to exceed the families' labor resources, they had to weigh in the added cost of the wage labor in deciding whether to increase output. The rising wages of agricultural workers in the latter half of the Tokugawa period posed a major disincentive.

By no means did all the advantages lie on the side of small-scale producers. Wealthy peasants could take greater risks and experiment with new techniques. Whereas small landholders often cultivated mulberries on scattered strips of land distant from the rearing site, large landholders could devote part of their holdings to mulberries and plant entire parcels, which greatly simplified plowing, mulching, and harvesting. Often, poor peasants could not afford to build special sheds for silkworm rearing, but had to use rooms in their homes. Since silkworms do best in light, airy rooms, the location and construction of the house might be such that conditions were not entirely advantageous. Nevertheless, labor-intensive production, use of family labor, and absence of costly investment as a prerequisite for using the best technology were factors that counterbalanced the advantages enjoyed by wealthy peasant producers. Ability and good fortune determined who would reap the profits. As a passage in yet another manual argued, ability counted most:

28. Kanō, p. 124.

There are good years and bad years depending on the weather, but one man gets better results than another, depending on his methods. Let two men be equally lucky, one will succeed and the other fail by reason of differences in skill. Even in good growing years, when everyone prospers, yields vary with skill.[29]

Sericulture and Peasant Economy

In addition to being labor intensive, sericulture was attractive to peasants because it was taxed at a very low rate. The *kokudaka* system, which fixed rents according to the acreage and productivity of registered parcels, dated from the late sixteenth century, when rice cultivation predominated, and assessments corresponded to traditional assumptions about land use. As a result, rice and cereal crops were taxed at a high rate, but not crops grown on unirrigated and comparatively infertile land. Often planted on uplands, waste areas, and the edge of rivers and streams, mulberries were lightly taxed. The labor value added in silkworm rearing, reeling and spinning, and egg card manufacture also escaped the full weight of the lord's fisc. In Shindatsu, the Bakufu levied a small tax on braziers used to boil cocoons; and at the end of the eighteenth century, villages specializing in egg card manufacture began to pay a yearly fee for permission to stamp their cards with a registered mark. But neither tax was large.[30] For the most part, sericulture was not taxed directly, and this undoubtedly contributed to its growth.

Because rearing silkworms did not require much land, it was especially attractive to peasants with small holdings. Large-scale producers devoted part of their agricultural holdings to mulberry husbandry, since cultivating and harvesting evenly planted stands was the only efficient way of tending so many trees. Small-scale producers used land around their homes, on levees, along paths and the borders of fields. If they planted an

29. Smith, "Ōkura," p. 140.
30. Araki Moriaki, "Yōsangyō no tenkai to Tokugawa ki no jinushi-kosaku kankei," in *Yōsangyō no hattatsu to kisei jinushisei* (n. 13, above), p. 138.

entire parcel with mulberries, they also planted between the rows—wheat and rape seed for a winter crop, and soy beans for the summer.[31] In terms of land use, then, sericulture did not compete directly with traditional crops, and, as we saw earlier, technological advances minimized conflicts with respect to use of labor. If satisfied to be small producers, poor peasants could engage in sericulture without reducing their investment in farming.[32] They might have to purchase leaves to supplement their own supply, but they could sell the cocoons two months after incubating the eggs.

Lightly taxed and land saving, small-scale silk production provided an invaluable source of income. It is no surprise that small producers far outnumbered large ones by the end of the Tokugawa period. Although there are few sets of quantitative data on peasant silk production in Shindatsu, we can use reports from two villages—Shimoōishi (1860) and Moniwa (1870)—which list the number of egg cards reared by each household (see table 5). Sericulture was not the primary occupation of the producers in these villages, and the data show the structure of silkworm rearing as practiced by peasants in order to supplement farm income.

Since rearing one card of silkworms required the full-time labor of two persons and most families were nuclear or stem families, rearing two cards or more usually involved hiring additional labor. The data indicate, then, that in both villages most peasants relied on family labor and limited production accordingly. Only 6 percent of producers in Shimoōishi and 4 percent in Moniwa reared more than one and a half cards; large-scale production accounted for just 21 percent and 13 percent of the villages' total. Clearly, small-scale production was dominant.

---

31. Furushima Toshio, *Nihon nōgyō gijutsu shi*, vol. 2 (Tokyo, 1949), p. 695.

32. A Bakufu official noted in a report written in 1768: "Being that this is an industry suitable for those who are elderly or infirm and incapable of field work, it is an important addition to the local economy." *Fukushima-shi shi*, vol. 2, p. 565.

TABLE 5. *Silkworm Rearing in Two Shindatsu Villages*

Scale of production	Number of households	Total cards
Shimō-Ōishi, 1860:		
¼ – ½ card	43.0 (50%)	11.5 (17%)
1 – 1.5 cards	38.0 (44%)	42.0 (62%)
2 or more	5.0 (6%)	14.5 (21%)
	86.0 (100%)	68.0 (100%)
Moniwa, 1870:		
¼ – ½ card	113.0 (61%)	56.5 (37%)
1 – 1.5 cards	66.0 (35%)	75.0 (50%)
2 or more	8.0 (4%)	19.0 (13%)
	187.0 (100%)	150.5 (100%)

SOURCE: For Shimō-Ōishi, *Fukushima-ken shi*, vol. 9, *Kinsei shiryō 2* (Fukushima, 1965), pp. 915–916. For Moniwa, *Fukushima-shi shi*, vol. 9, *Kinsei shiryō 3* (1971), pp. 73–77.

Most peasants who reared silkworms on a small scale harvested cocoons and raw silk, which they sold at local fairs and to itinerant buyers who came to the villages. Many large-scale producers, however, manufactured silkworm egg cards. Instead of boiling the cocoons, they hatched the moths, mated them, and collected the eggs. Manufacturing egg cards required additional weeks of work and overlapped with peak-demand periods in rice cultivation.[33] It also required highly skilled techniques and increased the risk of losing the crop due to human error and natural calamities. Egg card manufacturers tended to be well-to-do peasants who could afford to hire additional labor and accepted risks in the hope of realizing higher profit margins. But although large-scale production predominated in egg card manufacturing, producers confronted similar problems related to negative economies of scale. Small-scale production increased markedly in the late eighteenth and early nineteenth centuries.[34] The extent of the increase cannot be

33. Yoshida, *Satō*, pp. 132–145.
34. *Fukushima-shi shi*, vol. 3, pp. 383–385.

documented, but competition was sufficiently severe that several times villages which possessed patents to market egg cards petitioned the Bakufu to suppress the activities of unlicensed producers.[35] As had happened first in raw silk production, small-scale manufacturers using family labor steadily gained ground.

Sericulture was not the only source of nonfarm income, but the above data and ample literary evidence suggest that it played an important role in the local economy. Officials recognized that income earned by silkworm rearing allowed thousands of rural poor, who otherwise would have been forced out of agriculture entirely, to keep their status as peasants. In fact, the seigneurial class looked favorably on sericulture and encouraged its development, unlike cash crops such as tobacco and cotton which were thought to be detrimental to traditional farming.[36] The following observation by an official of Fukushima *han,* who in 1838 toured sericulture villages north of the castle town, shows why they approved:

> With respect to raising silkworms, if one visits the area one can readily see that landholdings are small and little profit can be realized from farming. Sericulture is thus essential for peasants to pay their taxes.[37]

The growth of by-employments and manufacturing in rural Japan during the last century of Tokugawa rule profoundly affected village social structure. The most remarkable change was the appearance of great numbers of peasants who owned little or no land and could not subsist by farming alone. Table 6 shows the distribution of land in three Shindatsu villages just before the Meiji Restoration. The villages represent three types of economy and development found in the district. Located in the plain, Yanagawa was a market village; it was also a major center of silkworm rearing and of producers specializing in egg card manufacture. Moniwa was a mountain village where many peasants

35. *Fukushima-ken shi,* vol. 9 (Fukushima, 1965), p. 907.
36. Furushima, *Nōgyō gijutsu,* p. 470.
37. *Fukushima-shi shi,* vol. 3, p. 380.

TABLE 6. *Landholding in Three Shindatsu Villages*

Holdings in koku	Number of households	Percent of village land
Yanagawa, 1863:		
30 plus	8 (2%)	38%
29.9–20	6 (2%)	13%
19.9–10	7 (2%)	9%
9.9–5	31 (9%)	18%
4.9–3	34 (10%)	11%
2.9–1	54 (16%)	8%
0.9–0	202 (59%)	3%
	342 (100%)	100%
Moniwa, 1870:		
30 plus	1 (0.5%)	5%
29.9–20	0	0
19.9–10	5 (2%)	9%
9.9–5	39 (18%)	39%
4.9–3	44 (20%)	23%
2.9–1	85 (38.5%)	21%
0.9–0	47 (21%)	3%
	221 (100%)	100%
Kitahanda, 1866:		
30 plus	2 (2%)	7%
29.9–20	3 (2%)	7%
19.9–10	38 (28%)	48.5%
9.9–5	42 (32%)	28%
4.9–3	17 (13%)	6%
2.9–1	15 (11%)	3%
0.9–0	16 (12%)	0.5%
	133 (100%)	100%

SOURCE: For Yanagawa, *Fukushima-ken shi*, vol. 9, *Kinsei shiryō 2* (Fukushima, 1965), pp. 716–728. For Moniwa, *Fukushima-shi shi*, vol. 9, *Kinsei shiryō 3* (1971), pp. 73–77. For Kitahanda, *Fukushima-ken shi*, vol. 9, *Kinsei shiryō 2* (1965), pp. 637–652.

worked in forestry and reared silkworms as a by-employment. Kitahanda, located in the foothills of the mountains at the northern end of the plain, was predominantly agricultural. The data reveal a direct relationship between development of commerce and by-employments and the proportion of households with small and marginal holdings. Generally, between five and three *koku* was the minimum needed for subsistence farming. The contrast between Yanagawa and Moniwa, on the one hand, and Kitahanda, on the other, is obvious: in Yanagawa and Moniwa, peasants with less than five *koku* were more than twice as numerous, and with less than three *koku* were three times as numerous, as in Kitahanda. Yet a striking difference appears with respect to the bottom stratum: 60 percent in Yanagawa and 21 percent in Moniwa had less than one *koku* of land. Either they were tenant farmers, or they supported themselves mainly by wage labor, handicrafts, and trade—in which case, although peasants by status, they did not live by farming.

The data on tenancy in Yanagawa, where marginal and landless peasants were most numerous, suggest that many of these families did not depend primarily on farming. In 1863, of the 113 village residents who owned no land at all (*mudaka*), only 56 rented farmland, and we do not know how much.[38] A considerable amount of the land in the village was rented to peasants from neighboring settlements, which suggests that Yanagawa peasants had alternative sources of income.[39] This is confirmed by data contained in a survey conducted in 1867 which listed the principal occupations of 284 households in the north ward of the village. According to the survey, only 106 households (37 percent) depended mainly on farming, of whom 18 were tenants. The most numerous nonfarm occupations were egg card manufacture (18), day labor (16), carpentry (12), and smithing

38. *Fukushima-ken shi*, vol. 9, pp. 716–728. The population register of the village indicates which landless households (*mudaka*) were tenant farmers, but not how much land they rented.

39. Morita Takeshi, "Bakumatsu Meiji shonen nōmin tōsō," in *Murakata sōdō to yonaoshi*, vol. 1, ed. Sasaki Junnosuke (Tokyo, 1972), p. 220.

(7). In addition, 31 households managed food shops: fish (9), bean curd (8), tea (7), sweets (6), sake (5), and rice (5). There were even four inns and two hairdressers.[40]

A market village located near a heavily traveled turnpike, Yanagawa was *not* typical of villages in Shindatsu. Also, the data are far from complete: we do not know in every case that income from occupations exceeded income from farming, though that is the presumption. Nevertheless, we can see that growth of commerce, manufacture, and by-employments such as sericulture brought about fundamental changes in economy and social structure.[41] Many peasant households in Shindatsu villages did not own enough land to subsist as self-cultivators; if they were not tenants, they depended on by-employments and wage labor for economic survival.

Throughout Japan in the late eighteenth and nineteenth centuries the development of commercial agriculture—producing for the market rather than for household consumption—brought about changes in land tenure as wealthy peasants accumulated land at the expense of small cultivators. Generally they leased newly acquired land to tenants, since farming large holdings required hiring additional workers at a time when wage labor had become costly. Not all of the land was rented out. Depending on the location and productivity of the parcel and the households' resources and needs, they might add to the land they cultivated. Nevertheless, the trend was toward leasing rather than expanding the scale of farm operations, and landlord-tenant relations, which had been rare before the middle of the eighteenth century, proliferated toward the end of the period.

Although closely associated with the development of commercial agriculture, loss of land by small peasants varied consid-

40. Shōji, *Yōsangyō*, pp. 102–103.

41. The following works by Thomas C. Smith contributed greatly to my understanding of economic change in rural Japan in the latter half of the Tokugawa period: *The Agrarian Origins of Modern Japan* (Stanford, Calif., 1959); "Farm Family By-Employments," *Journal of Economic History* 29, no. 4 (December 1969): 687–715; *Nakahara* (Stanford, 1977).

erably in degree, depending on the particular form that commercial agriculture assumed. The highest incidence of tenancy is recorded for cotton- and rice-producing villages, where land productivity also tended to be high. In the Kinai cotton districts, tenancy reached 70 to 80 percent, and in rice-exporting districts, such as the Shonai plain north of Fukushima, a few landlords owned whole villages. In contrast, silk-producing villages contained comparatively small numbers of tenant farmers, even though commercial farming had substantially supplanted subsistence farming.[42] Data on tenancy rates in Shindatsu during the Tokugawa period do not exist, but we can infer low rates from slightly later data. According to an 1883 government survey, less than 25 percent of farmland in Shindatsu was cultivated by tenants, and eight of ten farmers either owned all the land they farmed or owned and rented.[43] Land laws and tax reforms promulgated in the 1870s by the Meiji government disadvantaged small cultivators, many of whom lost all of their land during the 1881–1885 agricultural depression. It is safe to assume that in the late Tokugawa period tenancy rates in Shindatsu were even lower than the 1883 data indicate.

Three interrelated reasons account for the comparatively low rates of tenancy in Shindatsu. Land productivity was low, which limited the potential profit to be gained through the acquisition of farmland; being land-saving, sericulture did not in itself greatly increase demand for farmland; and sericulture provided an alternative to tenancy for families whose holdings were too small for subsistence farming.

As noted earlier, income from sericulture provided many poor peasants with cash to purchase essential foodstuffs. It is useful to consider a hypothetical case, even though the extent to which selling raw silk and egg cards supplemented house-

42. Ōguchi Yūjirō, "Bakumatsu ni okeru yōsangyō no hattatsu to nōson kōzō," *Tochi seidō shigaku* 19 (April 1963): 38–54; Arizumi Sadao, "Yōsan chitai no nōgyō kōzō," in *Bakumatsu ishin no nōgyō kōzō*, ed. Horie Hideichi (Tokyo, 1967), pp. 192–252. Ōguchi studied sericulture villages in the Shinshu region and Arizumi in the Kai region.

43. Ōishi Kaichirō, *Nihon chihō zaigyōsei shi josetsu* (Tokyo, 1961), p. 93.

hold food needs varied according to the relative prices of the commodities they traded, the amount they produced, and production costs. Data from the mid-nineteenth century show that peasants rearing one card, which was the norm in many villages, harvested approximately 400 *monme* (53 ounces) of raw silk.[44] Before the silk boom that followed the opening of Yokohama in 1859, this quantity would have sold for 2 to 3 *ryō* which, in turn, bought between 1.5 and 2.0 *koku* of rice. One *koku* was assumed to represent the yearly food needs of an adult male. Depending on production costs, a family of three adults and two children might purchase up to 25 percent of the food they consumed.

Income from sericulture filled the gap between what small cultivators produced in the way of foodstuffs and their subsistence needs. It is absolutely essential, however, to bear in mind that this income was highly volatile due to a number of factors, each of which profoundly affected peasants' ability to provide for their needs. To begin with, output fluctuated from year to year. Despite advances in mulberry husbandry and silkworm breeding, silk production remained vulnerable to various natural calamities, and at any point the peasant might lose the entire crop. In addition to variations in output, selling prices affected earned income. Though used widely by both samurai and better-off commoners, silk was a luxury good and demand was likely to fall during economically depressed periods, which was also when small peasants needed the income most. Prices of rice and other foodstuffs also varied from one year to the next, depending largely on supply. Thus, the exchange value of the silk was as uncertain as the bounty of the harvest. A peasant might lose half his crop one year and reap a bumper harvest the next, but if in the first case demand for silk was unusually high and supply low, and if rice prices were down, he might be able to purchase more food than in the second case. On the other hand, one can easily imagine how low output and high rice prices drastically reduced customary purchases.

44. The estimate of 400 *monme* per card of silkworms reared was calculated from data contained in *Fukushima-ken shi*, vol. 9, pp. 915–916.

The volatility of income in sericulture partly accounts for small producers' extensive reliance on short-term, high-interest loans. They borrowed to finance production costs, which principally involved the purchase of egg cards and mulberry leaves as needed to supplement home supply. The cost of such loans was high, but because the production cycle was short they could be repaid within a few months. Depending on resource and production needs, small peasants pawned movable property and land as security for the loans. It is impossible to estimate the extent of such loans, since only fragmentary data on usury in Shindatsu exist for the Tokugawa period. Literary references are plentiful, however, as will be seen in chapter 6, and there are data from a somewhat later period which support the inference that short-term credit played a major role in the peasant economy. According to a survey made in 1875, eight years after the downfall of the Tokugawa shogunate, moneylending accounted for 27 percent of the income of well-to-do peasant families in four representative Shindatsu sericulture villages. Land accounted for 33 percent—a measure of usury's importance.[45] Moreover, recent research on pawned land in sericulture villages of the Kai region confirms that where silk production predominated, mortgaged land was extremely common.[46]

The boom-bust character of sericulture apparently did not discourage small peasants; in fact, the great majority of these families reared silkworms. It is reasonable to assume that poor peasants were vulnerable to abrupt economic change. Since they frequently pawned even their land to finance production, one wonders why they assumed such risks. Here we must speculate, because the rural poor left few written statements which articulated conscious motivations. Two conjectures can be offered. First, precisely because of its boom-bust character, sericulture offered the best escape from low socioeconomic status. Research by Araki Moriaki on changes in landholdings among the egg-

45. Shōji Kichinosuke, *Yonaoshi ikki no kenkyū* (Tokyo, 1970), p. 34.
46. Arizumi, "Yōsan chitai."

card producers of Fushiguro village, Shindatsu, show that more than seventy percent of the households experienced radical changes in economic status during the period in the late eighteenth and nineteenth century when sericulture production prospered most.[47] Although one cannot equate size of holdings with wealth, or assume that loss of land was always involuntary, the data show that small peasants frequently rose to become substantial landowners, and some large holders lost most of their land. Second, the risks of failure must have been preferable to the alternatives. We saw that by rearing silkworms families could maintain their status as landholders, even though holdings were too small to subsist on. Without sericulture they would have had to hire out as day laborers, take up trade, or compete with similarly situated peasants for farmland. It would appear that neither day labor nor petty trade was likely to guarantee security, but either meant loss of the status of being landowners. To attempt to continue as farmers by renting land, however, meant competing for land which was generally ill-suited to growing rice and cereals—the traditional agricultural uses. And the competition, of course, would drive up rents.

In conclusion, some social effects should be noted. Because of the efficiency of family-centered silk production and the low capital requirements, poor peasants became silk producers, and the benefits and risks associated with being producers were distributed broadly. If the technology available in the Tokugawa period had allowed great economies of scale in sericulture, small producers could not have survived; and since average holdings were very small, marginal families would have been forced to work for large producers as wage earners. They would have become a rural proletariat.

To some extent this happened, as Sasaku Junnosuke forcefully argues.[48] Nevertheless, many were able to continue living

47. Araki, "Yōsangyō tenkai," pp. 127–130.
48. Sasaki Junnosuke, "Bakumatsu no shakai jōsei to yonaoshi," in *Iwanami kōza Nihon rekishi*, vol. 13 (Tokyo, 1975), pp. 247–299.

on their holdings because of income earned by rearing silk-worms. They were still farmers, even though agriculture did not provide subsistence needs. In this way, despite the growth of market relations, certain continuities with village life in the more purely subsistence economy of the early Tokugawa period persisted. Thus, it is unlikely that either the wealthy or the poor peasants fully realized the extent to which the market and the development of commodity production had created new conflict relations.

6. The 1866 Shindatsu Uprising

Wealthy peasants who witnessed the 1866 uprising in Shindatsu wrote the reports, letters, and personal histories of the uprising which are our main source of information.[1] The longest and most vivid account of the uprising, circulated without the author's name soon after 1866, began by enumerating the immediate causes: "Looking carefully into the origins of this disturbance, we see new taxes on raw silk and silkworm egg cards, thirty percent increases in interest rates, and extraordinary price increases, especially for rice and other cereals." The author used a rustic metaphor to suggest how each contributed to the outcome: the taxes on silk were the seed; inflation and higher interest rates germinated it; soaring rice prices served

1. My analysis of the 1866 Shindatsu uprising draws heavily on the research of Shōji Kichinosuke, especially *Yonaoshi ikki no kenkyū* (Tokyo, 1970), pp. 20–85. In addition, I made use of three documents relating to the uprising published by Shōji Kichinosuke and Aoki Kōji. The most complete account of the uprising is the "Oū shū Shinobu-gun Date-gun no onbyakushō shū ikki no shidai," an annotated text of which appears in *Minshū undō no shisō*, ed. Shōji Kichinosuke et al. (Tokyo, 1970), pp. 274–286; hereafter cited as "Ikki shidai." A second, "Ikki uchikowashi ni tsuki todokegaki," is in *Nihon shomin seikatsu shiryō shūsei*, vol. 6, ed. Aoki Kōji et al. (Tokyo, 1968), pp. 746–752; cited as "Ikki todokegaki." The third is "Shindatsu Keiō ninen sōdō jikki," ibid., pp. 758–765; hereafter cited as "Sōdō jikki."

as fertilizer; and the seedling soon grew into a tree with strong branches and luxuriant leaves.[2]

Each of the accounts of the uprising provides a different perspective, but all agree that the silk taxes were the immediate cause, and that a clique of local wealthy peasants, rather than the Edo Bakufu, should bear the burden of blame. We are told that "lowly persons proposed this tax, not our rulers," and further that these "rascals" had hatched a "wicked plot" against the government and common people.[3] The allegation that a small group of local peasants instigated the tax is intriguing because taxation was a ruling-class prerogative. How, then, did the hateful silk tax come into being?

In the early autumn of 1864, two wealthy peasants, Giemon and Bun'emon, spokesmen for a small group of large-scale silk producers in Shindatsu, wrote to the Bakufu intendant, Kawakami Itarō, stationed at Koori, the main Bakufu office in the district. They complained that large quantities of substandard silkworm egg cards were being manufactured locally, disrupting the market and damaging the reputation of established producers, and called for rigorous inspection to enforce the high standards needed to protect their trade. They asked that the Bakufu commission them to inspect locally produced silkworm eggs; proposed that, as inspectors, they collect the taxes on inspected cards; requested five-year appointments; and offered to pay a large sum for the franchise to serve as inspectors and tax collectors.[4]

Silkworm egg card manufacture was a highly complex occupation requiring great skill in every phase of production: harvesting the eggs, attaching them to cards, and storing the egg cards until sold. Compared with harvesting raw silk, which was widely practiced, egg card manufacturing traditionally had been concentrated in a score of villages which a century earlier had specialized in this aspect of sericulture.[5] Specialization in-

2. "Ikki shidai," pp. 274, 284.
3. Ibid., p. 274.
4. Shōji, *Yonaoshi,* p. 56.
5. Shōji Kichinosuke, *Meiji ishin no keizai kōzō* (Tokyo, 1954), p. 164.

creased the quality of the cards produced, and Shindatsu egg cards began to acquire a reputation for excellence. By the late eighteenth century, besides supplying local sericulturists, certain villages were selling cards to producers in other districts. In 1774, commercially ambitious manufacturers from Shindatsu petitioned for the right to use a special trademark (*honba*) authorized by the Bakufu.[6] The mark designated "established centers" of egg card manufacture; a patent was granted to only certain villages, and all producers in these villages could use the mark. They paid the Bakufu an annual tax, the cost of which was shared by individual producers in proportion to the number of cards manufactured.

By the 1830s there were more than twenty-five *honba* villages in Shindatsu, and they produced the great majority, though not all, of the region's silkworm eggs.[7] After the opening of Yokohama and the ensuing boom in silk exports, however, many more peasants started to manufacture egg cards. Because of inexperience, and in some cases because of fraud, egg cards of inferior quality were produced.[8]

Established manufacturers rightly feared the consequences of the sale of substandard cards. In contrast to marketing raw silk, the quality and weight of which were easily ascertainable, successful marketing of silkworm eggs depended to a large extent on reputation: only after the eggs hatched did the buyer know the precise number and species. Hence the marketing of inferior cards by some Shindatsu peasants was injurious to producers from chartered villages.

There appears to have been a legitimate basis for requests that the government intervene to enforce minimum standards. At first glance, the proposals outlined in the letter sent by Giemon and Bun'emon do not, contrary to the allegations of our chronicler of the 1866 uprising, seem to be the ingredients of a "wicked plot."

There is, however, sufficient evidence to suspect the motives of Giemon and Bun'emon; indeed the wording and timing of

6. *Fukushima-shi shi*, vol. 2 (Fukushima, 1972), pp. 570–571.
7. Ibid., vol. 3 (1973), pp. 462–464.
8. *Yokohama-shi shi*, vol. 2 (Yokohama, 1959), p. 522.

their letter to Kawakami are suspicious. The use of certain set phrases in the letter suggests that Giemon and Bun'emon had access to a document then circulating within the office of the Finance Magistrate which advocated, for the first time, employing wealthy peasants as agents to help in the regulation of the silk trade.[9] In fact, the similarities between the plan outlined in their letter and the government's plan for inspecting and taxing egg cards are too great to be coincidental. Moreover, intendant Kawakami showed surprising zeal in making the appointments. The Bakufu officially approved the plan and promulgated the regulations early in 1866, while in the late fall of 1864 Kawakami had already nominated the group headed by Giemon and Bun'emon to fill posts as egg card inspectors— posts that did not officially exist at the time.

It is not surprising that when Kawakami announced the plan and nominated the Giemon-Bun'emon group to be the inspectors, local egg card producers soon voiced objections. The first protest came from Fushiguro village, one of the original *honba* egg card villages in Shindatsu. On 12/18 (lunar calendar) in 1864, shortly after Kawakami's announcement, the headman and nine assistant officers petitioned against the new regulations. They did not deny the need for inspection and quality control, but impugned the motives of the Giemon-Bun'emon group, accusing them of "plotting to further their own selfish interests." The petitioners claimed that their village had always produced egg cards of superior quality and, therefore, did not need outside supervision: "We have been manufacturing silkworm-egg cards . . . for about a hundred years. We always paid the tax, and by specializing in this work attained a consistently high standard." Previously they had paid a yearly tax directly to the Bakufu. What they now objected to so strenuously was the proposed role of the Giemon-Bun'emon group. "We are dismayed and alarmed that, as part of the new policy, taxes must be paid directly to [these] individuals."[10]

The authors of the petition were themselves large-scale pro-

9. Ibid., pp. 462–464.
10. Ibid., p. 58.

ducers who annually manufactured and marketed from two hundred to four hundred cards, selling locally and in neighboring provinces.[11] They marketed their own cards and feared that the powers to be granted to the inspectors were more likely to be used against them than against the producers of substandard cards. They did not oppose either taxation or inspection per se, but did not trust the men who would obtain the franchises. As we will see, they went to great lengths to protect their rights.

Although Kawakami ignored the petition from Fushiguro, opposition to the plan mounted. During the next month, six more villages sent petitions opposing the appointments. Failing to persuade Kawakami, these villages brought together representatives who agreed to organize a new round of protests. Their activity alarmed Kawakami, who, in a conciliatory gesture, appointed a local notable in an attempt to mediate the dispute. But when the Giemon-Bun'emon clique refused to compromise, several of the villages resolved to petition directly to Kawakami's superiors at the office of the Finance Ministry in Edo. Fushiguro, Yanagawa, and Hobara villages each commissioned representatives who, one by one, began the long journey to the capital.[12]

Kawakami discovered the plan only after two of the three representatives had departed. Frightened that direct petitions would lead to an inquest, he immediately reversed his position of unconditional support of the Giemon-Bun'emon group and ordered that the two parties to the dispute reach a compromise, which they did in the spring of 1865. According to the terms of the settlement, Fushiguro and other villages that had expressed opposition promised to forego litigation; in return, the "chartered" egg card villages were to be allowed to pay taxes directly to the intendancy.[13]

The agreement settled the dispute that had begun six

11. Ōishi Shinzaburō, "Yōsan shijō ni tsuite," in *Yōsangyō no hattatsu to kisei jinushisei*, ed. Furushima Toshio and Takahashi Kōhachirō (Tokyo, 1958), pp. 319–325.

12. Shōji, *Yonaoshi*, p. 59.

13. Ibid., pp. 59–60.

months earlier over Kawakami's nomination of the inspectors. We know the protagonists and the terms of the settlement— but what were the real interests involved? In the first petition against the regulations, the headman of Fushiguro village denounced Giemon and Bun'emon for their "extraordinarily selfish desires."[14] Once again (and from a different source) we find allusions to a "wicked plot."

Six of the would-be inspectors—Giemon, headman of Nakaze village; Umaji, headman of Oka village; Bun'emon, assistant headman of Oka village; Banroku, headman of Nagakura village; and Kichijirō, chief headman, and Isaku, headman, of Koori village—are identified by name and position in various documents.[15] This information, meager as it is, tells us something about their likely economic interests and political connections. They were high-ranking peasant officials in villages that were directly involved in the manufacture and sale of silkworm-egg cards—Nakaze, Oka, and Nagakura ranked among the largest producers of egg cards in Shindatsu and hosted the most important silk market in northeastern Japan. This fair, held annually in June at the Atsutamyōjin and Gozutennō shrines in Oka and Nagakura, drew buyers from many parts of the country, and bidding at the fair established the prices of locally produced silk. As the headmen of Oka and Nagakura villages, Bun'emon, Umaji, and Banroku occupied a strategic position with respect to the Shindatsu silk market. Moreover, Kichijirō and Isaku, the top peasant officials in Koori, provided the link to Kawakami and Bakufu officials at Koori, for as the highest-ranking peasant officials they would be in daily contact with Bakufu personnel.

What can we conclude from the evidence presented? The Giemon-Bun'emon group petitioned for appointments through the patronage of intendant Kawakami with the intention of gaining leverage over the Shindatsu egg card market. When Kawakami indicated his approval of the plan, Fushiguro and other

14. Ibid., p. 58.
15. "Ikki todokegaki," p. 746; "Sōdō jikki," p. 759.

chartered egg card villages which feared that they would lose their autonomy as producers and middlemen strenuously objected and, by threatening to bring suit in Edo, forced Kawakami to compromise his support of the Giemon-Bun'emon clique, who, outflanked, made concessions.

The terms of the settlement reveal that commercial interests lay at the heart of the controversy. The principal concession demanded and obtained by the opposition was the right to pay taxes directly to the intendant, rather than to intermediaries. They also won the right to inspect cards manufactured in their own villages, and, as a final measure to ensure their autonomy, insisted that the names of the inspectors be removed from the inspection seals. They were willing to pay taxes—but only if allowed the freedom to manufacture and market their goods.

Up to this point, only wealthy silk producers from villages that specialized in egg card manufacture took an active part in the struggle. The disputing parties were village headmen and large-scale manufacturers of egg cards, not ordinary peasants, and were equally skilled in lobbying to further their interests. But we shall see that the opposition to inspection and taxation that came from small-scale and generally poor peasants proved to be much more intractable.

Poor Peasants Protest

Early in 1866, nine months after the first controversy was settled, the Bakufu finalized its plan for inspecting and taxing silk production. Soon after, the intendant's office at Koori promulgated the following edict.

> It has been brought to our attention that in recent years the silk market has been subjected to great disruption, causing untold hardship to the people. Henceforth, for the purposes of regulation, all producers, not only those in territories directly controlled by the Bakufu but also in small fiefs and temples and shrines, must have their products inspected at the office of the nearest intendant.

All raw silk, whether to be sent to Kyoto, used locally, or exported to foreign countries must be faithfully inspected and stamped. . . .

Concerning silkworm-egg cards, we recently heard that unauthorized persons have been producing and marketing silkworm eggs, causing great distress to producers. In order to regulate the trade, henceforth inspectors shall be appointed in both Bakufu and private fiefs to carry out the new policy. They will buy up the paper cards and after affixing seals distribute them to producers. The cards will thus be properly identified as to the name of the producer, place of origin and species. Silkworm-egg cards for export must be taken to the intendant's office, where additional tax money will be collected. Hereafter both raw silk and silkworm-egg cards must be stamped and certified before being sold, and any person who fails to comply with these regulations shall have his goods confiscated.[16]

The second round of protests against the plan began in the spring of 1866 when the regulations were put into effect. This time, small-scale silk producers were the moving force. The first protest was a petition from Fushiguro villagers who identified themselves as "middling and small peasants." Their chief complaint was the provision that the silk be inspected and taxed prior to sale. They explained that they did not have sufficient cash to finance all of their operating costs during the silkworm-rearing season, and were therefore forced to borrow from moneylenders: "Large and prosperous farmers are different, but we find that the procedures for inspection cause the most extreme difficulties. In order to pay for the food we eat, extra helpers, and mulberry leaves, we sell our silk, little by little, as soon as it is finished and at local markets; [we must also] pawn our possessions in order to carry on."[17]

The tax did not bother well-to-do peasants. To be sure, it was an added cost, but they had plenty of cash on hand. For small producers who were already in debt, however, the tax came at the worst possible moment. According to the petition, they had to sell the silk as soon as it was spun and reeled. But because of

16. Shōji, *Yonaoshi*, p. 62.
17. Ibid., p. 65.

the new regulations, they were now required to take their goods to the intendancy at Koori.

> During the silkworm-egg card harvest, nobody has a minute to spare, and if one falls behind for even a moment, losses will be enormous. If we are forced to take each day's production to the offices at Koori for inspection . . . we lose precious time. Even if we work day and night, our efforts will come to naught.[18]

The peasants went on to make a strong plea for repeal of the taxes and reinstatement of the old system under which villages paid an annual tax, reiterating the claim that their survival as small producers was at stake.

As happened eighteen months earlier when the village officers of Fushiguro protested, the intendant ignored the petition. But unlike the rich and well connected, small-scale silk producers did not have the resources required to take their complaints to higher authority. By themselves, poor peasants who could not even afford to pay the tax until they had sold their goods were incapable of mounting the kind of campaign needed to protect their vital interests. They needed the assistance of elite villagers—but none was forthcoming.

Petitions having failed, the peasants went underground. Soon messages began to circulate, passed from village to village according to a prescribed route. In one circular, they complained bitterly that the short supply of rice was due to hoarding and speculation on the part of wealthy peasants, and asserted: "It is now impossible to purchase rice, or even barter for it. Although young and old are at work tilling their fields, there is absolutely no hope in sight." They warned that people were beginning to take matters into their own hands. "Because everyone understands what is happening, when bonfires are lit it is a signal to hold meetings." Yet they felt it was still possible to persuade high-status peasants to join the movement, and advised peasants to enlist them in the struggle wherever possible. "If villagers are withholding support, go to them, discuss the issues with them, and make them understand."[19]

18. Ibid.
19. Ibid., p. 41.

Next they attacked Giemon, Bun'emon, and Kichijirō: "There are three men from Oka, Koori, and Nakaze villages who, obsessed with self-interest, established new procedures for collecting taxes on silk and silkworm-egg cards." Charging that the taxes imposed "great hardship throughout the district," they warned that patience was wearing thin, but did not rule out the possibility of a peaceful settlement, and in closing expressed the hope that "peace and abundance prevail throughout the land."[20]

Hopes for peace and abundance proved short-lived. At the height of the silkworm-rearing season and at a critical point in the rice crop, cold rain swept across Shindatsu. Stormy weather continued for several weeks and temperatures plummeted. At one point the weather cleared, but rain and cold soon returned, dashing hopes that the crops could be saved. Speculation and hoarding drove up prices, and peasants wanting to buy rice had to pay more than twice the previous year's price (and four times the price of 1863). Moreover, moneylenders raised interest rates by 30 percent, making it even more difficult to buy dwindling supplies of foodstuffs.

The uprising began with a boycott of the annual silk fair at Oka and Nagakura villages. Umaji, Bun'emon, and Banroku, three members of the original clique, were the headmen of these villages, and in protest against the taxes, peasants refused to attend the fair. According to one witness, they managed to shut it down: "Every year great crowds would come to the fair, arguing, jostling each other, rubbing shoulders. But this year not a single person came, making it a desolate place."[21]

The Uprising

Early in the evening of 6/15, the second day of the boycott of the silk fair, about fifty peasants gathered in Oka village. They lit bonfires, drummed on pots, blew conches, shouted,

20. Ibid.
21. "Sōdō jikki," p. 759.

shrieked, and whistled. More people came, carrying torches, staves, picks, hoes, axes, and shovels. They marched to the house of Umaji, the village headman and recently appointed silk inspector. As they circled the house, a leader stepped forward and shouted: "Be especially careful with fires! Don't spill and scatter rice! Don't carry off pawned goods, because they belong to other people! Don't steal money! This is being done to help the people, not for selfish reasons. But smash everything in this man's house, even the cat's dish."[22] Whereupon they fell upon the house, knocking down the doors and screens; they stormed inside and smashed everything in sight. Nobody was hurt, but Umaji's property lay in ruins.

That evening they attacked Bun'emon, the assistant headman of the village; Banroku, the headman of neighboring Nagakura; and the other inspectors who lived in the area. After the first attacks, the leaders drafted a manifesto which they circulated throughout the district.

> Acting selfishly and avariciously, Umaji of Oka village, Banroku of Nagakura, and six others have turned their backs on the hardship they cause the people by collecting taxes under the new system. This year crops have been poor, and many silkworms did not spin proper cocoons. Just when everyone was struggling to eke out a living, the new regulations were put into effect. Now we cannot even market our goods, and the poorest are on the verge of starvation. Several attacks have already occurred, and greater disturbances are imminent. We will not tolerate the calamity that is upon the land.[23]

The text was written on a thick sheet of paper of the type used in egg-card manufacture, and around the message were the names of seventy-four villages.[24] Each village which received the circular marked its name and sent it to the next destination. This way the peasants knew which villages had withheld support. To them they sent runners carrying the following message.

22. "Ikki shidai," p. 275.
23. "Sōdō jikki," p. 759.
24. "Ikki shidai," p. 284.

Our purpose is to aid poor and impoverished people, and therefore everyone must lend support. If you refuse, we will gather a
great force and descend on your village, set fires, and burn everything down.[25]

The leaders planned to mobilize peasants from every part of
Shindatsu, march on Koori, and demand cheap rice and cancellation of the silk taxes. To enlist the maximum number of peasants, instead of proceeding directly to Koori, which was only a
few miles from Oka and Nagakura, they set out on a three-day
march. Starting on 6/17, the crowd, which had assembled on
the west bank of the Abukuma River, crossed over and
marched north through villages on the east bank. They
drummed up recruits and demanded food and drink from
wealthy villagers and, if refused, laid waste their property. Late
that afternoon they reached the northern end of the valley, re-
crossed the river, and entered Isazawa, where they carried out
five attacks. The first victim was a prosperous moneylender,
Shishido Kisōji, whose pawnshop they ransacked, "pulling out
everything and throwing the goods into rice fields where they
trampled them into the mud." Even sacred objects were not
spared. Suspecting that he hid money under the household
shrine, they knocked it down, dug up the foundations, and
rifled the cache buried underneath.[26]

In all, there were seventeen raids on the third day of the uprisings, five more than in the first two days. Most of the targets
were pawnbrokers and merchants, but some were headmen
who withheld their support, as in the case of Hanzawa
Heishichi, the headman of Nishiokubo village. The peasants
went to his house to demand that he join the march to Koori.
They made repeated appeals, but Heishichi feared association
with the uprising more than he feared the peasants confront-
ing him. Angry and frustrated, they destroyed his home.[27]

An influential headman who refused to lend support to the
demonstration became the object of a particularly furious attack.

25. Ibid., p. 274.
26. "Ikki todokegaki," p. 746.
27. Ibid., p. 749.

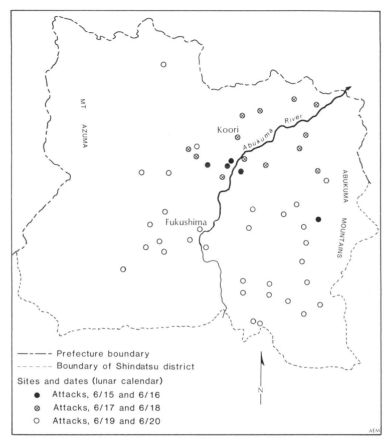

Map 3. *Uprising in Shindatsu District, Fukushima Prefecture, 1866*

Late in the evening of 6/17, a group of peasants set out for Kita-handa village, the home of Hayata Dennosuke. Dennosuke was the supervisor of Bakufu silver mines at Mount Handa and chief of the surrounding villages, and had close connections with Ba-kufu officials in Koori and Edo. The peasants were well aware of his influence, for several years earlier he had used his connec-tions in the capital to reduce the *sukego*—corvée labor along turnpikes—quota assigned to the villages under his administration.[28] His wealth, prestige, and connections made Dennosuke the ideal spokesman. But perhaps because he was unsympathetic, perhaps fearing the consequences of association, he fled before the crowd reached his house. The enraged peasants destroyed everything they could lay their hands on. They broke into his house and storerooms and "carried out all kinds of household property, pawned goods, clothing, bedding, and cushions until not a thing was left."[29] They smashed his sumptuously decorated shrine to the harvest god and dug up the family gravestones. They split casks of miso and sake, and broke into the granary, spilling and scattering many bushels of rice.

On 6/18, the fourth day, the peasants finally coerced several headmen from villages near Koori to march with them, carrying banners calling for the cancellation of the silk taxes. By this time rumors of the march had spread to villages which the crowd had not actually visited, and many thousands of peasants converged on Koori, the home of Kichijirō and Isaku, and the site of the Bakufu office. Kichijirō attempted to protect the town by erecting barricades, but the peasants quickly broke through and immediately attacked the homes of Kichijirō and Isaku and several merchants. They also broke into the jail and freed three peasants who had been arrested on the first night of the uprising, as well as a number of common criminals.[30]

Next they marched to the Bakufu office. They arrived to find that Itakura Naizenshō, daimyo of Fukushima *han*, had sent a hundred well-armed soldiers to defend the headquarters. The peasants were largely unarmed, and the sight of serried ranks of riflemen, mounted warriors, and even a cannon brought them to a standstill.

There is some disagreement as to what happened next. According to an obviously fictionalized account, Lord Itakura himself rode forth and demanded an explanation. Three leaders stepped forward and, "trembling from head to toe," com-

28. Ibid., p. 747.
29. Ibid.
30. Ibid., p. 748; "Ikki shidai," p. 277.

plained of terrible hardship caused by soaring rice prices and taxes on raw silk and egg cards. While apologizing for their riotous behavior, they pleaded that they could not live another day. In reply, Lord Itakura conceded that they had valid grounds for making appeals. Only the Bakufu could rescind the taxes, he noted, but since "peasants faced starvation" he ordered the taxes suspended on his own authority. He also ordered lower rice prices.[31]

Lord Itakura's appearance at Koori and the exchange with the peasant leaders are not mentioned in any of the other accounts of the uprising and can be dismissed. Nevertheless, all of the documents report that Lord Itakura, upon learning of the uprising, sent out horsemen who posted placards announcing the suspension of the taxes and substantial reductions in rice prices and interest rates.[32] The confrontation at the intendancy, however, was much less dramatic: when the crowd reached the headquarters, they were dispersed by a single volley fired over their heads.[33]

After marching on the intendancy, the crowd, which up to that point had maintained a degree of common purpose and discipline, ceased to be a coherent force. Breaking into a score of smaller groups, the peasants attacked and pillaged wealthy villagers. The number of raids rose from 29 in the first three days, to 43 on the fourth day, and 96 on the fifth day.[34] Rich peasants tried to save their homes by providing food, drink, and even clothing. Some of the stories of measures taken to curry favor are fantastic, though the reporter insisted that the following incident was told to him by eyewitnesses. An extremely well-to-do peasant clad himself and his family in formal attire and stood outside his gate bowing and nodding like an unctuous proprietor greeting favored customers. Inside, his relatives and servants scurried about pouring cups of sake and heaping food on plates, continually urging their guests to eat

31. "Ikki shidai," pp. 277–278.
32. See "Sōdō jikki," p. 763; "Ikki shidai," p. 278.
33. "Ikki todokegaki," p. 748.
34. Shōji, *Yonaoshi*, pp. 43–51.

and drink their fill. They used only the most deferential language, and at the first sign of displeasure prostrated themselves and poured forth effusive apologies.[35]

It was more common for moneylenders, landlords, and merchants to post notices listing generous donations of rice and cash to help the poor. Many households advertised their good deeds well in advance of direct threats to their property, but some who waited until the last moment found themselves bargaining with a crowd poised to attack. A few well-to-do peasants even engaged priests to negotiate on their behalf. During the first days of the uprising, property smashings had been planned attacks. The leaders directed the crowd from village to village, and within each village moved from house to house, following lists prepared in advance. But in the last days, after the movement had lost its direction, houses were attacked at random. Many peasants became drunk on looted sake and behaved like common thieves. Some property smashings were said to have been the work of vagrants, masterless samurai, and gangsters who passed themselves off as peasant leaders, prompting one observer to pun that the uprising was not a gōso (mass demonstration) but a gōtō (violent robbery).[36] Households gave rice and money to one group of rioters, only to be confronted later by an entirely new group. One resourceful man profited from the confusion by writing the word "settlement" on a sheet of rice paper and attaching it to his portal. When he heard that peasants were approaching his house, he put on a headband and stripped to a loin cloth to blend in with the crowd. Just before they reached his house, he ran to the front and pointing to the paper shouted, "This house has been done! Let's go on! Let's go on!" The crowd was fooled and continued on its way.[37]

The fifth and penultimate day of the uprising was the most violent—96 raids in 37 villages. Geographically, the raids, heretofore concentrated in sericulture villages in the northern

35. "Ikki shidai," p. 276.
36. "Ikki todokegaki," p. 749.
37. "Ikki shidai," p. 282.

half of the valley, spread to every corner of the district.[38] But even before the uprising reached its apogee, the ruling class began to assert its authority, as in Lord Itakura's well-publicized order suspending the taxes and mandating price reductions. At the same time, daimyo of fiefs bordering on Shindatsu sent large contingents of samurai. From the east and south, Sōma, Miharu, and Nihonmatsu sent three hundred each; from the north, Yonesawa sent five hundred, and Shiroishi a hundred. There were no reports of clashes between samurai and the rioters. Apparently the threat of force was sufficient to discourage further attacks. The uprising ended on 6/20.

The uprising did not alleviate the economic pressures on the peasants. The Bakufu overruled Lord Itakura and continued to collect taxes on raw silk and silkworm-egg cards.[39] Once order was restored, wealthy peasants refused to sell rice for anything less than what the market would bear. Because much rice had been destroyed during the uprising, prices actually increased. Peasants who had pawned raw silk, cloth, and other valuables as security for loans received at most half-compensation for goods stolen or damaged. Moreover, many moneylenders refused to extend credit (or were unable to), which greatly slowed recovery.[40]

An uprising caused by hardship apparently created even greater privation. And looking solely at the immediate effects, one of the chroniclers concluded his account with a rude simile to sum up the result of peasant's violence: It was like a cow defecating in its own water; it benefited not even itself.[41]

Economic Background

In addition to political and social factors, economic distress clearly motivated the peasants. The manifestos circulated be-

38. Shōji, *Yonaoshi,* pp. 47–51.
39. Ibid., p. 67.
40. "Ikki shidai," p. 282.
41. "Sōdō jikki," p. 764.

fore the uprising and the subsequent accounts written by wealthy peasants cited rapid increases in rice prices as the cause of acute, widespread distress. But the magnitude of the impact on the peasants' livelihood is not yet clear. At the very minimum two factors—rice and silk prices—must be considered, because the peasants' ability to purchase food was largely a function of the exchange value of these commodities. Still, not all the peasants depended to the same extent on selling silk and buying rice. One should also assess the importance of sericulture to various strata of landholders, especially the middling and small peasants whose rage appeared boundless. Finally, it is necessary to look more closely at the period immediately preceding the crisis to understand what the peasants' expectations might have been.

When in 1859 the Bakufu concluded treaties opening Yokohama to trade with the West, raw silk was Japan's most avidly sought commodity. The signing of the Commercial Treaties coincided with worldwide shortages of the fiber. The long-term cause of the shortage was a silkworm blight which for two decades plagued producers in France and Italy. Starting in southern France in 1840, it reached a peak in 1852 when European output was less than one-tenth of normal.[42] At the same time the Taiping rebellion (1851–1864) disrupted silk production and trade in southern and central China, further restricting world supply. Thus, when Japan opened its doors to foreign trade, merchants from all over the world rushed to Yokohama to buy silk.

Between 1860 and 1868 Yokohama merchants alone exported slightly more than 15 million pounds of raw silk, an amount estimated to equal the total output during the previous decade.[43] The increase in demand naturally had an immediate impact on prices. In Shindatsu, for instance, the account books of a wholesale merchant named Tsudu show that in less than a year the price of a bale of top-quality raw silk rose from 75 ryō to

42. *Yokohama-shi shi*, vol. 2, pp. 378–379.
43. Ibid., p. 395.

TABLE 7. *Wholesale Prices of Rice and Raw Silk in Shindatsu, 1854–1866*

Year	1 to of rice	Index	100 monme of raw silk	Index
1854	.40 *ichibu*	84	.49 *ryō*	92
1857	.48 *ichibu*	100	.50 *ryō*	94
1859	.55 *ichibu*	115	.59 *ryō*	111
1860	.87 *ichibu*	181	.95 *ryō*	179
1861	.67 *ichibu*	140	.97 *ryō*	183
1862	.74 *ichibu*	154	.80 *ryō*	151
1863	.83 *ichibu*	173	1.31 *ryō*	247
1864	—	—	—	—
1865	1.61 *ichibu*	335	1.85 *ryō*	349
1866	3.33 *ichibu*	694	2.38 *ryō*	449

SOURCE: Morita Takeshi, "Bakumatsu Meiji shonen no nōmin tōsō," in *Murakata sōdō to yonaoshi*, vol. 1, ed. Sasaki Junnosuke (Tokyo, 1972), pp. 211–246. I add the index (based on prices in 1854, 1857, and 1859) to indicate prices before the opening of Yokohama.

125 *ryō*. "The market is in a most extraordinary condition," Tsudu wrote in his diary in November 1859. A month later he added, "Never before have such prices been recorded."[44]

While foreign merchants and the Japanese merchants who acted as middlemen surely reaped the greatest profits, the unprecedented surge in demand forced wholesalers to bid up prices at regional markets where peasants sold their goods. With the exception of weavers, who suffered from the export of the raw materials needed to practice their craft, everyone in Shindatsu involved in the silk trade profited at first. The prosperity was partly checked, however, by other forces. Rampant inflation was caused by the Bakufu's increased minting of debased gold and silver coin.[45] According to one estimate, between 1860 and 1869

44. *Fukushima-shi shi*, vol. 3, p. 544.
45. Peter Frost, *The Bakumatsu Currency Crisis* (Cambridge, Mass., 1970), p. 35.

the money supply increased two to three times, and it did not take long for commodity prices to catch up. In Edo, for instance, salt which sold for thirty *monme* per *koku* in 1860 cost sixty in 1864, and one *shō* (1.9 quarts) of lamp oil, which cost five *monme* in 1860, cost nine in 1864.[46] Inflation eased at the end of 1863, but in Shindatsu and many eastern provinces rice prices rose due to restrictions on internal trade ordered by the Bakufu in preparation for the first punitive expedition against rebellious Chōshū *han*, the leading fief in the movement to restore imperial rule. The next year, bad weather caused widespread crop failure which accelerated price increases.

Data on wholesale silk and rice prices compiled by Professor Morita Takeshi and reproduced in table 7 show that in the decade prior to the opening of Yokohama, rice and silk prices fluctuated within a relatively narrow range. But between 1860 and 1864 the price of silk rose more rapidly than that of rice, due to surging exports. Compared with the period from 1854 through 1859, silk rose 94 percent and rice 62 percent. During the next two years the price of rice quadrupled while that of silk did not even double, showing that peasants' purchasing power fell precipitously prior to the uprising. The figures do not, however, indicate how the decline affected various strata among the peasant population.

The data on household silkworm rearing and landholdings come from a single village, Moniwa, the only village in Shindatsu for which these data are available.[47] Table 8 shows that 85 percent of the households engaged in sericulture as a farm by-employment. All of the nonproducers had less than five *koku* of land; but, by comparing producers and nonproducers according to holdings *and* family size, one sees that family was the key variable. Table 9 shows that even among households with marginal holdings, 75 percent of the households with four or more members, and all with eight or more, reared silkworms. Large families with comparatively small holdings—1 to 3 *koku* and 3 to 5 *koku*—had an even higher ratio of producers.

46. Sasaki Junnosuke, "Yonaoshi no jōkyō," in *Kōza Nihon shi*, vol. 5 (Tokyo, 1975), pp. 102–103.

47. *Fukushima-shi shi*, vol. 9 (Fukushima, 1971), pp. 73–77.

TABLE 8. *Silkworm Rearing, Moniwa, 1870*

Silkworm-rearing households	176	85%
Non-rearing households	32	15%
Total	208	100%

SOURCE: *Fukushima-shi shi*, vol. 9, *Kinsei shiryō 3* (Fukushima, 1971), pp. 73–77. Only those households positively identified in the 1867 census have been included.

TABLE 9. *Family Size and Silkworm Rearing, Moniwa, 1870*

Family size	Rearing households	Non-rearing	Percentage of rearing households
A. Holdings under 1 *koku*			
Small (1–3 persons)	3	9	25%
Medium (4–7 persons)	21	7	75%
Large (8 or more persons)	4	0	100%
All households	28	16	64%
B. Holdings under 1–3 *koku*			
Small (1–3 persons)	9	7	56%
Medium (4–7 persons)	40	4	91%
Large (8 or more persons)	16	0	100%
All households	65	11	86%
C. Holdings of 3–5 *koku*			
Small (1–3 persons)	3	1	75%
Medium (4–7 persons)	25	3	89%
Large (8 or more persons)	10	1	91%
All households	38	5	88%

SOURCE: *Fukushima-shi shi*, vol. 9, *Kinsei shiryō 3* (Fukushima, 1971), pp. 142, 146, 184; ibid., vol. 8, *Kinsei shiryō 2* (1968), pp. 486–527.

We should not be surprised by these findings. Precisely because they farmed small plots, large families were likely to have more hands than were needed in traditional agricultural activities. If they could rear silkworms without reducing agricultural output, the raw silk and the egg cards represented a pure gain in labor productivity; and we have seen that mulberries could be grown on land that was less than ideal for cereals. Even if not self-sufficient in mulberries, they could purchase additional leaves as needed, provided they could buy on credit. Table 10 presents combined data on the size of holdings and the number of cards reared by each stratum. It shows that the ratio between the number of cards reared to land owned was highest *for peasants with the least land.* The data do not indicate whether the land was used for cereal or cash crops, nor do they tell us how much land the households farmed as tenants (or rented out). Nevertheless, it is reasonable to suppose that the smaller the family's holding, the greater was the need to buy food. In the extreme case—that is, comparing households holding less than one *koku* with the largest landholders—the ratio was nearly ten times as great. Comparing households with less than five *koku*, the ratio was still three times as great. And peasants with less than five *koku* made up 73 percent of the silk producers in Moniwa.

TABLE 10. *Landholdings and Silkworm Rearing, Moniwa, 1870*

	Average holding, in koku	Average number of cards reared	Ratio, cards/koku	Index
Less than 1 koku	.66	.64	.97	606
1–2.9 koku	1.88	.65	.35	218
3–4.9 koku	4.02	.75	.19	119
5–9.9 koku	6.69	1.05	.16	100
Over 10 koku	24.02	2.50	.10	63

SOURCE: *Fukushima-shi shi*, 9:73–77; 8:486–527.

We can conclude that one of the forces in the 1866 Shindatsu uprising was the "price-scissors" effect, as the poorest suffered the greatest reduction in purchasing power relative to essential needs. Moreover, rearing silkworms entailed cash outlays for eggs and often for extra leaves. Peasants borrowed to finance production costs, and many pawned land and valuables as security, anticipating profits from selling the silk. The margin between success and bankruptcy was slight. In the spring of 1866, extraordinary rice prices, bad weather which reduced the silk output, and the burdens of new taxes and inspection procedures together threatened the small producer with disaster.

Mobilization in the Late Tokugawa Period

More is known about the men presumed to have plotted the Shindatsu uprising than what they did in their capacity as leaders. The moving spirit behind the protests, if not the actual organizer, was Kanno Hachirō of Kanaharada village, Shindatsu. Fifty-six years old at the time of the uprising, Hachirō had already acquired renown as a moralist, philosopher, and political activist deeply concerned about national and local politics.[48] After the arrival of Admiral Perry's gunships brought pressure from the West that Japan open its ports and establish diplomatic relations, Hachirō petitioned the government, urging the construction of blast furnaces (to produce iron for armaments) and improvements in coastal defenses, and fraternized with zenophobic, anti-Bakufu samurai in nearby Mito *han* who advocated the overthrow of the shogunate and a return to direct rule by the emperor. Arrested by the Bakufu in 1858, he returned to Kanaharada, where he organized a society to instruct villagers in the virtues of sincerity, filial piety, and strict morals, and in stick fighting, which together would serve to fortify them spiritually and physically against bands of ruffians who infested the area. He also petitioned the govern-

48. Shōji Kichinosuke, *Kinsei minshū shisō no kenkyū* (Tokyo, 1979), pp. 210–211.

ment against official malfeasance and the corrupt practices of village headmen.[49] In view of these facts, it appears likely that he was instrumental in organizing the protests which culminated in the uprising. Unfortunately, there is no way of knowing the extent of his involvement. Immediately after the uprising he went into hiding, and subsequently he denied having played any role at all.[50] Having been imprisoned once, he was a likely suspect, and one can probably discount the denial. But even after the overthrow of the Bakufu he stuck to his story. A second leader identifiable from contemporary sources is Michimaru, formerly a peasant from Sendai, who had settled in Shindatsu after he was expelled from his native village. The circumstances surrounding his expulsion are unclear; all we know is that after leaving Sendai he moved to Shindatsu, where he married a widow and made his living teaching stick fighting.[51]

Neither Hachirō, a rustic, self-trained intellectual and political activist, nor Michimaru, a man expelled from his native village, possessed the kind of status that the leaders of peasant movements traditionally enjoyed.[52] More importantly, the people who customarily represented the collective interests of villagers were conspicuous by their absence. Village officials consistently refused to speak to the needs of poor peasants, and in doing so they violated the norms of peasants' collective action established early in the Tokugawa period. Despite changes in their economic relationships due to the growth of the market, the peasants in Shindatsu still expected, even demanded, the support of village officials. Circulars issued before the uprising urged headmen to take up their cause; and in preparation for the march to Koori, the crowd made repeated efforts to enlist particularly influential headmen, who refused even token support. Instead of uniting high and low in opposition, peasant mobilization in Shindatsu actually exposed all the more sharply the cleavages produced by differing economic status and conflicting interests.

49. Ibid., pp. 223–224; Shōji, *Yonaoshi*, pp. 39–40.
50. Shōji, *Minshū shisō*, p. 223.
51. "Ikki todokegaki," p. 749.
52. Sasaki Junnosuke, *Yonaoshi* (Tokyo, 1979), pp. 109–110.

If high-status peasants did not join, types not previously involved in peasant movements were conspicuous.[53] All accounts
mention that people who were not farmers—masterless samurai, migrant laborers, peddlers, vagrants—played an active
role. They appear to have been most prominent in the last days
and perhaps were, as some have insisted, responsible for the
thinly disguised looting that predominated after the march to
the Bakufu intendancy.[54] Yet the reports are not sufficiently
specific to distinguish the actions of such persons from those of
local peasants, or to assess their role and influence. It is enough
to note their presence. Economic development had proceeded
to the point that persons other than peasant farmers were part
of the rural population. And as the society became ever more
complex, so did participation in protest movements. The
crowds were not only socially heterogeneous; they were also
much larger than in earlier movements. Peasants from every
part of Shindatsu, whether their villages were administered by
the Bakufu or by daimyo, joined the uprising to protest against
the silk taxes and rice prices—issues which transcended feudal
political jurisdictions. Every peasant who depended on sericulture was affected by the new system of inspection and taxation,
and any peasant who needed to buy rice desperately desired
that it be made available.

The size of the crowds and the extent of the violence were
without precedent in the history of the area. Though it is not
entirely clear how large these crowds were, the report that seventy thousand marched on Koori is surely a gross exaggeration,
since the total population was only twice that figure.[55] The estimate of between ten and twenty thousand is more likely, though
even this figure may be too high.[56] We do know the extent of the

53. Sasaki attributes the special character of violent peasant movements in
the late Tokugawa period to the widespread participation of the rural poor—
artisans, migrant laborers, tenant farmers, and villagers who had lost all or
most of their land. Being economically marginal, they welcomed *rōnin* (masterless samurai), gamblers, and the like as leaders of peasant uprisings.
54. "Sōdō jikki," p. 764.
55. Many scholars quote this figure uncritically.
56. "Ikki todokegaki," p. 748.

damage done. Among the many documents on the Shindatsu uprising published by Professor Shōji Kichinosuke is a report which lists the name, date, and village of every household raided.[57] Altogether, 184 homes and businesses—pawnshops, sake breweries, warehouses, granaries, stores—were hit in 63 villages. Destruction was complete. Furniture, clothing, and cooking utensils were demolished, in addition to commercial property. In the case of the very wealthy, losses were enormous. To take a single example, Saitō Shoemon of Ogura village listed the following: his house; stockrooms of sake, miso, vegetable oil; a silkworm-rearing shed and three outbuildings; three vats for sake brewing, three for making miso, and fourteen for soy; 600 silkworm-egg cards; 500 *ryō* in cash; and pawned goods valued at 1,600 *ryō*.[58] Even at the very high rice prices of that year, the goods destroyed equaled in value 400 *koku* of rice, which was enough to feed an entire village for the better part of a year.

It is not surprising that rich peasants who witnessed the destruction were appalled. Barrels of sake, soy, and vegetable oil were rolled out and split open, making rivulets in the dusty streets; bales of rice were wantonly looted, the peasants spilling as much as they carried off; peasants were reported to have defecated into vats of miso, so that neither the contents nor the tubs could be used again.[59] The victims were naturally outraged, and they were uncomprehending. "Now if we consider that scarcity of rice caused great hardship and induced them to riot, why would they waste the food in this way? Even if complete fools, they would not take revenge on food itself."[60] The writer concluded that they had lost their senses entirely.

The same author, a headman named Saburōzaemon, was certain of the "crazed" peasants' motives. "They had come to hate men of property and simply wanted to reduce them to utter poverty."[61] He does not, however, ask why they had come to

57. Shōji, *Yonaoshi*, pp. 43–51.
58. Ibid., pp. 71–72.
59. "Ikki todokegaki," p. 764.
60. Ibid.
61. Ibid.

hate the rich, thereby implying that hunger and misfortune naturally made people spiteful, envious, and mean. Other commentators probed more deeply. A rich peasant whose house was demolished in the uprising felt that the peasants had just cause. His harshest remarks were directed against the speculating rich who had refused to sell grain: he likened moneylenders who had raised interest rates in the midst of dearth to "leeches in paddy fields who live by sucking the peasants' blood."[62] They cheated the peasants, he charged, by confiscating pawned valuables before the expiration date of loans and never offering a fair price to begin with. But because they bribed officials, "Even when the evidence is against them, they always win in court."[63]

Being ubiquitous, the meanness of usurers and the stratagems and tricks of merchants do not in themselves explain what happened. The critical event in the Shindatsu uprising was one which the compassionate chronicler never mentioned—the repeated failure of village officials to protect the interests of the poor. If the peasants had attributed their suffering exclusively to the machinations of the Giemon-Bun'emon clique and the Koori intendant, very likely the protest would have taken a different course. In view of the wholesale abdication of responsibility by high-status peasants, and their refusal to lend even token support to the appeals of poor peasants, it is not surprising that the initial series of attacks escalated into a general onslaught against men of property.

From the beginning, criticism of the rich had been essentially moral. Broadsheets circulated before the uprising accused the inspectors and tax collectors of being "obsessed with self-interest" and thereby causing great hardship. The manifesto published after the first attacks justified the raids on the grounds that the elite peasants had turned their backs on the people's suffering. In the first days of the uprising, the leaders tried to enforce discipline in order to demonstrate that they,

62. "Ikki shidai," p. 285.
63. Ibid.

unlike their enemies, were not out to line their pockets. And because the cause was righteous, they felt entirely justified in compelling others to join, as seen in the circular which ordered each village to raise recruits. It also demonstrated the assertion of communal values over individual interests. Crowds looted in the last days of the uprising, but it seems very likely that the plundering of wealthy households was instigated by persons from outside the community. In principle, the peasants compelled the rich to donate rice and cash to "help the poor." The formality is significant, even if the result was similar. The peasants did not act blindly and their intention was not simply to "make the rich destitute." The morality they sought to impose had specific antecedents in the ongoing political values of anti-feudal peasant movements, according to which peasants shared a common, economically precarious fate as a powerless subordinate class whose only real hope for mitigation of hardship lay in collective response to crisis.

Before the extensive development of market relations, the survival of small peasants depended on seigneurial benevolence. Consequently, their economic problems were amenable to political solutions, and all strata of landholders within the village shared a material interest in pressuring the authorities to pay attention to their needs. But the growth of the market economy, so evident in sericulture districts, undermined the interdependence of villagers as a political community. We have seen that village officials did not act to protect the poor, first with respect to the new taxes and inspection system, or later to prevent hoarding of rice. Lacking the political connections and sophistication of upper peasants, as well as their financial power, small peasants mobilized around norms validated by the historical experience of peasants' struggle for survival. These were the only political resources they controlled, and they used them with a vengeance.

7. *Yonaoshi* Uprisings in Aizu, 1868

Conditions that contributed to peasant mobilization in the Aizu region in the autumn of 1868 included inflation, shortages of food, and disruption of trade, as was the case in Shindatsu two years earlier. Yet for the most part the suffering of Aizu peasants was not due to their dependence on the market. Rather, the immediate cause of distress, and the impetus to action, was the campaign mounted by the Imperial army against the forces of daimyo Matsudaira Katamori, one of the very few Tokugawa vassals who resisted the Meiji Restoration. During the month-long campaign the contending armies requisitioned food and horses, conscripted peasants to do corvée labor when they were about to harvest their crops, and laid waste fields and buildings that were in the line of battle. Anticipating a long campaign, the Imperial forces imposed a blockade, thereby aggravating the food shortages by preventing imports.[1]

In preparing for the assault on Aizu, the Meiji government made a modest attempt to win over the common people. Handbills distributed by the army's propaganda agents exhorted them to "work exhaustively" for the Imperial cause because the emperor "considers all the people to be his children."[2] The bills

1. *Aizu-Wakamatsu shi*, vol. 5 (Aizu-Wakamatsu, 1966), pp. 199–202.
2. Ibid.

also promised that villages which supported the war effort would receive substantial reductions in the land tax. Once they entered Aizu, however, government soldiers ruthlessly seized food, animals, and goods. Though the army issued orders forbidding improper treatment of the local population, the rape and rapine of the Imperial soldiers became legend: village women were sexually assaulted, even abducted and taken captive, and merchants came from as far away as Shirakawa, three days' journey to the south, to buy and barter war booty.

It is not surprising, therefore, that with the exception of a small number of peasants, most of whom were from the village headman class, few villagers volunteered their services to either army; neither did they lament the defeat of the Aizu army nor cheer the victory of the Imperial force. But the peasants were not blind to the significance of the collapse of the established political order and the opportunities that this presented. Indeed, a short ten days after the fall of Aizu-Wakamatsu, an uprising by the peasants of Takiya department, Ōnuma district, set in motion a series of local revolts that erupted in various departments *(kumi)* during the next three months.

On 10/3 (lunar calendar) of 1868, some two thousand peasants assembled at Gojōjiki village in mountainous Takiya department, southwest of Aizu-Wakamatsu. During the next several days they marched as a crowd to at least twenty villages, and in each they demolished the homes and property of the village headman and local moneylenders and merchants. Having finished with the attacks, representatives from each of the villages that joined the uprising assembled to consider a series of resolutions calling for radical changes in land tenure, debt relationships, and village leadership.[3]

The uprising in Takiya department did not spread immediately to other areas of Aizu. Although it set the pattern for subsequent uprisings, the action was planned and organized as a local movement rather than as the first stroke of a domain-wide upris-

---

3. *Aizu nōmin ikki shiryō shūsei,* ed. Tashiro Shigeo (Aizu-Wakamatsu, vol. 2 1978), p. 314; hereafter cited as *Aizu ikki.*

ing. The crowd did not carry out attacks in villages outside Takiya department, and elsewhere in Aizu peasants deliberated before taking action in their own communities. Twelve days elapsed before the next round of attacks, which occurred some distance away, in the vicinity of Aizu-Wakamatsu. The attacks began on 10/15 in Arai village in Kita-Aizu district and in the Takahisa department of neighboring Kawanuma district. Next, we see the uprisings moving in an arc north to Kitakata and east to the Inawashiro region at the foot of Mount Bandai, in the northeast corner of Aizu. One week after the last attacks were recorded in Inawashiro, violence erupted in distant Minamiaizu, in the extreme southwest. Beginning on 10/28, there were uprisings in four neighboring departments of Minamiaizu—Matsukawa, Narahara, Koide, and Yagojima—and subsequent uprisings in the Ina region from 11/2 to 11/9.[4]

The timing and location tell us something of the character of the uprisings, which were widely dispersed geographically and separated by long intervals, facts which show clearly that peasant violence did not spread by "contagion." They also suggest that there was little or no prior consultation between the leaders of local actions. Rather, in each department the peasants decided when to act and what action to take. Nevertheless, it is possible to speak of the many local uprisings as a single movement which followed the pattern of collective action set by the peasants of Takiya department: systematic destruction of the property of wealthy, high-status villagers and the subsequent convening of popular assemblies for the purpose of authorizing the reform of political and economic relations within local communities. To understand the scope of "world rectification," or *yonaoshi*, the term the peasants used, we need to examine both the attacks and the effort to bring about lasting change. In every case the first action of the peasants was to attack village headmen and other well-to-do villagers. A report filed by a group of headmen from the Inawashiro region described the attacks with which poor peasants began the work of *yonaoshi*.

4. Shōji Kichinosuke, *Yonaoshi ikki no kenkyū* (Tokyo, 1970), p. 119.

Suddenly, without any warning at all, from 10/19 to 10/22, peasants gathered from all over Inawashiro. Raising war cries, blowing on conchs, and clanging cymbals, they charged into our houses. They attacked homes, storehouses, and granaries; they cut down the roof supports, ripped up the tatami and floorboards, scattered our stores of rice, split open barrels of miso and soy sauce, and snatched up and burned land and tax records and other documents. They filled their sleeves with valuables; they even threatened our lives.[5]

The attacks followed the pattern of Tokugawa-period "smashings" (*uchikowashi*). The leaders and most of the crowd were members of the village community, although they might be joined by drifters, *rōnin*, and itinerant laborers; the choice of whom to attack was made in advance and the reasons for the attack were well understood; a large crowd was mobilized, if need be by threat, to demonstrate the collective nature of the violence; and the immediate purpose was to destroy the property of the rich and confiscate pawned goods, mortgage deeds, debt vouchers, and tax records. Planned days in advance, if not weeks, the uprisings usually took the victims completely by surprise, and the furious outpouring of pent-up hostility profoundly shocked the village headmen in particular, for they were accustomed to thinking of themselves as the benevolent guardians of these very people.

As in most of the violent uprisings of the late Tokugawa period, the smashings represented peasants' temporary rejection of traditional status and power hierarchies. In the Aizu uprisings, however, the peasants went one step further and attempted to change the village-leadership and economic relationships through which the elite dominated local society. The significance of the attacks will become clearer when we consider how the peasants used their new found power. We shall pay particular attention to the resolutions adopted by local assemblies, for they contain specific and practicable reforms that spoke to the needs of non-elite peasants. Documents made available through the extensive research of Shōji Kichinosuke

5. *Aizu ikki,* p. 322.

will be used, along with other records, to identify the conflicts that led to the attacks and also the aims and aspirations of the peasants who seized power at the local level.[6]

On 10/28, peasants from a number of villages in the Narahara department of Minamiaizu met to draw up a list of resolutions which defined the aims of their movement. (1) *Yonaoshi* was a matter to be decided by each department. (2) All village officials should be replaced. (3) All the old land records and other village documents should be confiscated. (4) Small cultivators should be allowed to serve as chief headmen. (5) With the exception of land, which was to be dealt with separately, all pawned goods should be redeemed without interest in five-year installments, starting from the current year, and the goods themselves should be returned immediately. Land tenure was a matter to be deliberated upon by each department. (6) Cash loans should be repaid without interest in ten-year installments starting from the current year. (7) A meeting should be held on 11/6 at Yubara, to which each village was expected to send two representatives.[7]

In other localities peasants convened assemblies and passed resolutions to give concrete expression to their aims. Documentation of the meetings is spotty, coming from only five or six of the assemblies. A comparison of these materials reveals differences in the specific solutions proposed, but more importantly they reveal a concurrence of interest in several principal issues. They were concerned with the proper constituency of collective action, reform of village government, settlement of pawned goods and outstanding debts, and solutions to problems related to mortgaged land and debt tenancy.

As in the attacks against high-status peasants, the convening of popular assemblies occurred at the department level. Departments were administrative precincts whose boundaries were drawn early in the Tokugawa period. Each department contained lands with an official assessed output of 10,000 *koku*,

6. Shōji, *Yonaoshi*, pp. 118–121.
7. *Aizu ikki*, p. 360.

which in most areas represented twenty to thirty villages. In all, there were 29 departments in Aizu proper and 27 in Mina-miaizu which the daimyo of Aizu administered on behalf of the Tokugawa house.[8]

The significance of the assemblies appears to be twofold: through formal (if temporary) organizational structures the peasants gave popular sanction to the changes they wished to carry out and mobilized support from all of the villages in the department. The degree of organization shows that they pos-sessed greater political sophistication and understanding of power relationships than is commonly ascribed to Tokugawa peasants.[9] There is, however, no evidence that they attempted to mobilize beyond the department. The small cultivators who carried out the movement in Aizu were not the parochial rus-tics who according to lore "knew nothing beyond the village hedges," but they were apparently not capable of organizing a domain-wide movement. Perhaps they did not see the need.

The most radical action of the Aizu peasant movement was the wresting of village office from hereditary headmen. Unlike the economically more advanced rural areas of Japan where by the latter half of the Tokugawa period the election or rotation of the head village office had supplanted family succession, in Aizu the office passed from father to son within the oldest and wealthiest household in the village.[10] The rule by hereditary succession was strictly enforced by the fief, which also granted headmen the right to have surnames and to bear arms—privi-leges normally reserved for members of the warrior class. Headmen possessed great power over the political and eco-nomic affairs of the village because they were the sole individ-uals qualified to represent the community in political appeals and financial transactions: the headman kept all village finan-

8. *Tōhoku shohan hyakushō ikki no kenkyū*, ed. Shōji Kichinosuke (Tokyo, 1969), p. 8.

9. Shōji, *Yonaoshi*, pp. 120–121.

10. Professor Andō Seiichi pointed out to me that the persistence of hered-itary village headmen in northeastern Japan may help to explain the wide-spread occurrence of *yonaoshi*-type movements in the Fukushima area.

cial records, assessed and collected taxes and dues, sponsored all petitions and civil suits, mediated controversies within the community, and exercised magisterial powers in a wide variety of village affairs.

The wholesale ousting of headmen shows that small cultivators were dissatisfied with the system of village government in which political authority was the patrimony of the family that boasted the longest lineage and possessed the largest fields. They chose, moreover, to replace the old headmen with their social peers. Data on the holdings of the former headmen and those who came to power after the uprising reveal that the mean holding of the old headmen was 25 *koku*, compared with 12 *koku* for the new village leaders.[11] The difference was more than a difference in relative wealth. In Aizu 12 *koku* represented the average household's holding and the amount of land that a family could cultivate with its own labor. To cultivate a 25-*koku* holding, on the other hand, required tenants, hired seasonal labor, or the services of household servants and poor relatives who were still economically dependent on the main branch of the family. Thus, the taking of office by the new headmen marked the transfer of local political power to a class representative of the majority of the village community, and the process through which they came to power revealed a new concept of representation sanctioned by popular assemblies rather than by the decrees of the ruling class.

In addition to attacking the authority of the traditional village leaders, the assemblies attempted to legislate more just economic relations. Their main concern was usurious short-term credit and the frequent loss of land and property as a consequence of peasants' inability to repay high-interest loans. Not all the proposals were the same, but without exception the assemblies demanded the immediate return of pawned goods. In Takiya department and in the Ina region of Minamiaizu they ordered the return of movable property without any compensation to the pawnshop owner; in Narahara, also in Mina-

11. Shōji, *Yonaoshi*, pp. 130–131, 135.

miaizu, peasants acknowledged the obligation to repay the principal of the loan but not the interest. Some variation can also be seen in resolutions dealing with outstanding debts. The Ina assembly canceled all past debts; the Takiya assembly canceled debts of more than two years' standing and ordered that other debts be repaid in installments over a ten-year period; the Narahara assembly ordered that all debts should be repaid without interest over the next ten years.[12]

The resolutions distinguished between mortgaged land and movable property. There was a broad consensus with respect to the treatment of pawned goods, but greater difference when it came to the land problem. Consistently the most radical, peasants in the Ina region of Minamiaizu ordered that the land be returned to the former owners. In Takiya department, however, the land was to remain in the possession of the mortgage holder and the rent to be canceled for one year. In Narahara, as noted earlier, the resolution simply stated that each department should decide questions related to land tenure. The intended meaning and the practical consequences of this are not entirely clear. Shōji Kichinosuke argues that the peasants intended to return to the original owners all land lost through unredeemed loans. Like many fiefs in the Kansei (1789–1801) period, Aizu followed the lead of the Bakufu in undertaking economic reforms to combat the growing power of the merchant class, and passed laws to restrict rural commerce and land accumulation by wealthy peasants. As a legacy of Aizu's Kansei reform movement, each village kept two sets of land records. One showed the holdings as recorded in 1813 when the domain attempted to equalize village holdings, and the other recorded the transfer of land through purchase and foreclosure. Shōji suggests that the peasants confiscated land records with the intention of restoring to the holders of record in the 1813 surveys those parcels of land that had been lost through foreclosure.[13] Except for the resolution passed by the assembly in the Ina region, however, there is little positive

12. Ibid., p. 122.
13. Ibid., pp. 122–123.

evidence, and it does not appear that land redistribution was actually carried out.

Meiji officials and troops stationed in Aizu did not immediately intervene to suppress the movement. Some of the uprisings took place far from government troops. But even where soldiers were billeted nearby, as in Inawashiro, they did not attempt to protect the headmen or punish the attackers.[14] Recognizing that the goals of the movement were strictly local, they were more interested in creating a new administrative apparatus than in adjudicating intravillage disputes. When thirty-seven ousted headmen from Takahisa department petitioned for reinstatement, they were told that it was not an opportune time to make changes since the villages were busy collecting taxes. They were also told that the new headmen had not proven themselves to be delinquent in the performance of official duties or to be guilty of improprieties.[15]

The hereditary headmen did not abandon their efforts to regain office. At the village level they employed various stratagems, ranging from acts of public repentance to bribery and a barrage of civil suits.[16] They also campaigned at the department level to persuade the Meiji authorities to reinstate them, boasting that "because of generation after generation of service to the lord of this domain, we are knowledgeable in the ways of controlling peasants."[17] They received strong support from the gōgashira, chief headmen who supervised the day-to-day administration of the departments. Unlike the headmen, the gōgashira had early been reappointed by the Meiji authorities, for without their assistance it would have been extremely difficult to carry out normal government functions.[18]

The political struggle for control of village office reflected the sharp division within the peasant class between the old wealthy farm families and moneylenders and the majority of

14. *Aizu ikki*, pp. 332–333.
15. Shōji, *Yonaoshi*, p. 145.
16. Ibid., p. 157.
17. Ibid., p. 120.
18. Ibid., p. 143.

small proprietors. If the old headmen desired to protect their economic interests in the village by regaining office, the resistance to their campaign showed an equally strong desire on the part of poor peasants to protect their recent gains.

The struggle also revealed an ideological clash between competing notions of what constituted the legitimate basis of local authority. The authority of the new headmen rested on the collective act of ousting the old headmen and convening assemblies to give popular sanction to the election of new officials, that is, community sanction. The old headmen relied upon an entirely different set of norms to justify the claim to being the rightful representatives of the village. They admitted without apparent embarrassment that the new headmen served "in accordance with the wishes of the villagers."[19] But they argued that their families' history of service to past rulers of the fief and their paternalistic concern for the welfare of the peasants made them uniquely qualified to serve as headmen:

> There are among us both ancient and more recently established lineages, but the great majority of us have ancestors who settled the villages and in this way came to serve as headmen. They were appointed to this office by the former lords of the domain, and for generation after generation the sons have been appointed to carry out the office. . . . Following the customs of old, we devoted ourselves to reclaiming fallow land and to increasing the number of people and horses within the realm. Though insufficient, we devoted ourselves wholeheartedly to the duty of nurturing the peasants under our rule.[20]

The small proprietors and poor peasants of Aizu violently repudiated the notion that the traditional economic and political hierarchy in the village adequately protected their vital interests. The peasants did not go one step further and attempt to "rectify" the larger relationship between themselves and their new rulers. Nevertheless, implicit in their actions was rejection of benevolence—the assumption that the obligation of

19. *Aizu ikki*, p. 332.
20. Ibid., pp. 332–333.

superiors to render benevolent attention to the needs of their charges transcended class interests. When the institutions of daimyo rule disintegrated before their eyes, the peasants of Aizu seized the opportunity to reform village government and legislate changes in economic relationships designed to protect their interests as small proprietors.

The "world" of the revolutionary peasant movement in Aizu was the village and not the state. When the peasants petitioned the Meiji authorities, the form and content of their appeals were entirely traditional—as if their relationship to higher authority had not changed at all. Examination of these petitions shows that they stayed well within the bounds of traditional peasant appeals. They asked for tax reductions because of the poor harvest, the devastation of crops, and the requisitioning of food; they requested changes in the procedures for tax collection to prevent speculation by middle-level officials; they appealed to the government to abolish monopolies on wax, lacquer, and other special products; and they demanded compensation for the services they rendered to the Imperial army.[21] In essence, they made the same kind of appeals to the Meiji government that they were accustomed to making to feudal lords.

The peasants attempted to implement radical changes at the local level. As would be expected of a bold assertion of rights, the resolutions adopted by the popular assemblies were declarative sentences, such as: "Nanushi yaku . . . subete tatekae" (all headmen . . . shall be replaced).[22] But in accepting the authority of the Meiji government, the peasants appear to have assumed the same political and psychological posture toward the new state as they had toward seigneurial authority. The petitions were rendered in the subjunctive, such as: "Onengu no gi, tō ikka nen wa nengunashi ni osetsukekudasaretaku" (It is [our] hope that [those above] will order the suspension of taxes for one year).[23] They still looked to the state for benevolence.

21. Shōji, *Yonaoshi*, pp. 120–121.
22. *Aizu ikki*, p. 360.
23. Ibid., p. 361.

Even though the *yonaoshi* movement in Aizu occurred at the very moment when on the national level Japan was shedding its feudal past, there were precise limits to "world rectification." It was a revolt by small cultivators and the poorer members of the village community against high-status peasants. They did not directly question their relationship to the state. Their concerns were local and not national, so that the peasants who sacked village officials and convened popular assemblies also appealed to the Meiji government for benevolence.

8. Conclusion:
Subsistence and Rebellion at the
End of the Tokugawa Period

In recent years scholars in the field of peasant studies have debated the relationship between subsistence crises and peasant
rebellion. In particular, James C. Scott, taking E. P. Thompson's
concept of the moral economy which informed the actions of
English crowds in the eighteenth-century food riots, has developed a comprehensive theory of peasant rebellion based on peasants' collective fears of famine and starvation. According to
Scott, because of the ever-present threat of famine, first and foremost peasants seek to guarantee subsistence needs, and consistently choose low-risk economic arrangements over potentially
more profitable ones which entail higher risks; further, peasants'
economic behavior as safety-first risk-avoiders ultimately ex-
plains their political behavior. Scott argues that exploitation per
se does not produce rebellion, since peasants perceive their interests in terms of "what is left" after paying rents and taxes,
rather than "how much is taken away." Peasants are likely to rebel
only when landlords and the state push them below subsistence
levels, that is, when faced with starvation. Thus, peasant collective action is characterized by desperate attempts to defend or
restore traditional subsistence-guaranteeing arrangements
which are being destroyed by market relations imposed from
outside.[1]

1. James C. Scott, *The Moral Economy of the Peasant* (New Haven, Conn.,
1976).

Scott's model contains at least two conceptual problems. The concept of subsistence, originally introduced as sheer physical survival, is soon broadened (as it must be to work empirically) to include culturally defined minimum levels of physical *and* social needs, that is, an acceptable standard of living. Hence, the model loses much of its analytic power as the link between peasants' economic and political behavior is attenuated. Second, it is by no means clear that peasants prefer subsistence-type economic relationships, or that "traditional" economic arrangements offer greater security. In an alternative interpretation of Vietnamese peasant movements provocatively titled *The Rational Peasant: The Political Economy of Rural Society in Vietnam,* Samuel Popkin has challenged Scott's major premise. Instead of doggedly holding the market at arm's length in order to minimize risk and guarantee subsistence, peasants choose market relations because even small peasant farmers can (and do) profit from commercial agriculture. Rather than something forced on peasants from outside, production for the market is the choice of peasants who calculate the probable benefits. Hence, economically peasants are rational; so, too, is their political behavior. Popkin argues that empirical analysis of peasant movements will show that they undertake political mobilization for the purpose of maximizing power within a given sociopolitical context. Peasant rebellion should not be interpreted as a purely defensive response to change.[2]

Peasant movements in the late Tokugawa period show that subsistence and violent protest were linked, although not as Scott's model would predict. The largest and most violent peasant movements occurred in sericultural districts like Shindatsu, where, within the last century, production for the market which centered around silkworm rearing had supplanted a more purely subsistence mode of production.[3] In these villages even small peasants depended on the market for their food needs.

2. Samuel L. Popkin, *The Rational Peasant* (Berkeley and Los Angeles, 1979), pp. 32–82.
3. Sasaki Junnosuke, "Yonaoshi no jōkyō," *Kōza Nihon shi,* vol. 5 (Tokyo, 1970), pp. 106–107.

Because of inadequate agricultural holdings, they bought much of their food with the cash they earned by selling raw silk and silkworm eggs. When successive years of crop failure, speculation by merchants, and widespread hoarding by rich peasants caused astronomical increases in rice prices, the poor went hungry. Confronted by a market-induced "crisis of subsistence," the peasants protested in force: they demanded that the government mandate low prices, and they physically compelled merchants and wealthy peasants who had been hoarding rice to make "donations" needed to "rescue impoverished people." In other words, they asserted the prior claims of the community to local supplies at a time when the market denied them food, and the obligation of the well-to-do to protect the minimum needs of its members.

But what can we conclude from the fact that small-scale silk producers caught in an acute "price-scissors" crisis made demands based on the idea of peasants' right to subsistence? The peasants' behavior and slogans clearly show their disavowal of the aberrant workings of the market and the upholding of collective and moral claims over individuals' rights to property. There is not, however, any evidence that they rejected market relationships as a totality. At no point did their actions indicate the desire to restore patterns of landholding and exchange that characterized the subsistence economy of the early Tokugawa village. Rather, they took from a political culture which had evolved in a pre-market feudal political economy such norms and values as could be used to mitigate immediate hardships. They used the ideological resources at hand in an attempt to minimize new risks. One lesson to be learned from the study of Tokugawa peasant movements is that "moral economy" political behavior, that is, protests and demands made in the name of the right to subsistence, do not necessarily, or even probably, imply a desire to return to earlier modes of production. The peasants understandably wanted protection within the new relationships.

We should also note that the theory of "rising expectations"—which holds that people who have become accustomed to more will rebel when it appears they will get less—provides little insight into the causes of rural conflict, even though the external economic conditions in Shindatsu at the time of the uprising show sudden economic reversal followed by violent collective action.[4] To some extent the development of sericulture and related by-employments improved the economic status of small peasants. The improvement was largely due to "self-exploitation," or increased output per household, as peasants chose to increase labor inputs at the expense of leisure.[5] Yet in considering the economic background to the Shindatsu uprising it must be remembered that silk production, for the great majority of the peasants engaged in it, did not alter their status as small producers who, year after year, lived precariously close to the edge of socioeconomic survival. Participation in the market as sellers of raw silk and silkworm eggs offered better prospects than simple subsistence farming. But it is erroneous to assume, as some economic historians have implied, that the real gains were sufficiently great to guarantee a margin of freedom from the daily struggle to provide necessities.[6] If anything, the Shindatsu uprising shows that peasants who combined farming and small-scale commodity production enjoyed very little security, and that the gains to be realized through "self-exploitation" were small. Hence, when the market turned against them, they suffered severely and felt their very existence as independent producers to be in jeopardy. Rather than discontent due to rising expectations, the uprisings point out the extreme vulnerability of these small peasants within the prevailing relations of production.

The uprisings in Shindatsu and Aizu were only two of the many large-scale rural disturbances in the last years of Tokugawa rule. From 1860 to 1869, a decade that began with the opening of Yokohama to overseas trade and ended with the final defeat of pro-Tokugawa forces, there were 484 peasant

4. Crane Brinton, *The Anatomy of Revolution* (New York, 1938), pp. 29–36.
5. The concept of "self-exploitation" is developed in A. V. Chayanov, *The Theory of Peasant Economy* (Homewood, Ill., 1966).
6. Susan B. Hanley and Kozo Yamamura, *Economic and Demographic Change in Preindustrial Japan, 1600–1868* (Princeton, N.J., 1977), pp. 19–28.

protests *(hyakushō ikki)*, and an additional 353 village disturbances *(murakata sōdō)* which did not directly involve the seigneurial class.[7] The great majority of peasant protests, 345, or
71 percent, occurred between 1866 and 1869, a period characterized by crop failure, rampant inflation, and the visible collapse of the Tokugawa hegemony. The level of violence that
accompanied peasant collective action also rose. Just six weeks
before the Shindatsu uprising, for example, women of Nishino-
miya, in Settsu, went to the local grain merchant to demand
cheap rice and triggered an outburst which engulfed hundreds
of villages around Osaka and parts of the city itself. The rioting
lasted two weeks and destroyed the property of 866 wealthy
commoners.[8] The next month poor peasants from Kaminaguri
village in the Chichibu district northwest of Edo led attacks
against four rice dealers in a nearby market town, the first of
450 raids in several hundred villages.[9]

Above all, the peasant uprisings in Shindatsu and Aizu at the
end of the Tokugawa period testify to the intensity of conflict
within the peasant class. Later I shall comment on the differences
between the movements in Shindatsu and Aizu, but here I am
concerned with their essential similarity. In both cases poor peasants mobilized not to overthrow feudal political structures,
whose collapse was imminent, but to attack village officials and
other wealthy peasants. What one sees, therefore, is a dramatic
shift in the social character of conflict, for in the early Tokugawa
period socially homogeneous and politically unified peasant
communities typically mobilized to oppose intensified seigneurial exploitation. But by the late Tokugawa period the intensity of
conflict within villages and between the various strata of the peasant class superseded conflict between ruler and ruled. When
peasants mobilized under crisis conditions they turned inward:
collective action took the form of property smashings and not
political action against the ruling class.

    7. Aoki Kōji, *Hyakushō ikki sōgō nenpyō* (Tokyo, 1971), app., p. 36.
    8. Sasaki Junnosuke, *Yonaoshi* (Tokyo, 1979), pp. 73–74.
    9. Patricia Sipple, "Popular Protest in Early Modern Japan," *Harvard Jour-
nal of Asian Studies* 37 (December 1978): 273–322.

Several long-term developments account for the distinctive pattern of late Tokugawa rural conflict. First, as we have seen, tax extraction failed to keep pace with increases in agricultural output. Here the role of structural factors should be noted, particularly the *kokudaka* system through which the seigneurial class appropriated rural surpluses. The Tokugawa daimyo depended on land rents, and, as William Roseberry has observed, "Rents, whether labor, kind, or cash, are inefficient since claimants do not control (or control indirectly) the means of production. Thus, adjustments to capture more of the surplus will be slow."[10] As absentee landlords, Tokugawa daimyo had additional problems since their retainers resided permanently in castle towns. Under these conditions, traditional peasant movements achieved considerable success in preventing increases in the land tax commensurate with gains in productivity. Collective action by peasants also checked many, though not all, attempts by the seigneurial class to tax the by-employments and trade of farm families. Hence, the *relative* weight of feudal taxes decreased. Second, production for the market increased stratification. In terms of juridical status all were peasants; but by the late Tokugawa period those at the top of the market economy were deeply involved in trade, moneylending, and renting land—competitive economic relations with other peasants. On the other hand, those at the bottom engaged in a type of subsistence farming to the extent that income from cash crops and by-employments was used "directly towards the purchase of subsistence goods."[11] Unlike subsistence farmers of the early Tokugawa period, however, for their survival they depended on the exchange value of the commodities they produced rather than seigneurial benevolence. In fact, there was little that even the most benevolent daimyo could do to protect them, for he could not regulate the economic behavior of thousands of individual participants in the market. The interest rates moneylenders charged, how much rice village merchants sold

10. William Roseberry, "Rent, Differentiation, and the Development of Capitalism among Peasants," *American Anthropologist* 78 (1978): 51.

11. Ibid., p. 54.

and at what prices, and the rents demanded by landlords were beyond the regulatory powers of the feudal ruling class.

To summarize, by the middle of the nineteenth century long-term changes in the rural economy had created severe disconti-nuities between the everyday reality of peasant life and ideal, ideological conceptions of social relations as defined by the feu-dal political economy. How, then, was collective action affected by the political upheavals that led to the Meiji Restoration?

The arrival of Commodore Matthew Perry's fleet of gun-boats in the mid-1850s and the subsequent signing of diplo-matic and commercial treaties which authorized trade and in-tercourse with the West gave groups hostile to Tokugawa rule the opportunity to demand its overthrow. Aided by antiforeign, pro-emperor zealots from many parts of the country, radical samurai in Chōshū, a powerful fief in southwestern Japan, twice challenged the Tokugawa Bakufu's military power. Their first revolt, in 1864, was defeated, but two years later the sho-gun could not mobilize sufficient support from his hereditary vassal daimyo and direct retainers to defeat a much smaller but highly motivated and well-equipped Chōshū army. The victory of Chōshū in 1866 ended more than two and a half centuries of Tokugawa hegemony. It could not be resurrected; the only question was who would now rule.

The ensuing struggle for national power—fought intermit-tently, and more frequently with proclamations than bullets—was carried out almost entirely within the warrior class. In Jan-uary 1868 a coalition consisting mainly of young samurai from Chōshū and Satsuma and a few Imperial court nobles an-nounced to a hastily assembled conference of daimyo the "res-toration" of the emperor and proceeded to rule in his name. Forces loyal to the shogunate fought two short and unsuccess-ful battles on the outskirts of Kyoto, the Imperial capital, and subsequently retired to Edo. Contingents of the domain armies of Chōshū, Satsuma, Tosa, and Hizen, now marching under the Imperial standard, pursued the retreating Tokugawa forces at a leisurely pace and reached Edo without having to fight a sin-gle serious battle. Soon after, the shogun Tokugawa Keiki

(Yoshinobu) peacefully surrendered Edo and ordered his retainers to lay down arms. Only a few domains in the northeast resisted the new government, among them Aizu whose defeat in the autumn of 1868 all but ended the brief civil war.[12]

The defeat of the 1866 expedition against Chōshū precipitated a revolutionary situation, a state of affairs which Tilly succinctly defines as the "onset of multiple sovereignty."[13] During this period peasant movements occurred in unprecedented numbers and, generally speaking, were larger and more destructive than at any previous time. The coincidence of national political upheaval and widespread peasant revolts raises again the question of the character of peasants' collective action.

The 1866 Shindatsu uprising was typical of peasant movements at the end of the Tokugawa period in that the peasants did not demonstrate militant antifeudal consciousness. Huge crowds of poor peasants destroyed homes, warehouses, and pawnshops, but they did not attack the centers (or even the symbols) of seigneurial rule and seize power themselves. They marched on the Bakufu intendancy at Koori to make specific, limited demands which were related to the exigencies of their immediate situation. Perhaps they were more skeptical of the efficacy of appeals to higher authority, for they did not retire peacefully after Lord Itakura ordered price reductions and the repeal of the silk taxes. The timing of the uprising—the Bakufu's armies were in the southwest, poised to attack Chōshū—may indicate that they were aware of the government's weakened position. But there is absolutely no evidence of revolutionary strategies and goals: neither attempts to forge alliances with anti-Tokugawa samurai bands, nor new organizational structures capable of challenging the military power of the samurai class.

Nevertheless, there were some changes in peasants' political consciousness, for some of the movements appropriated the

12. W. G. Beasley, *The Meiji Restoration* (Stanford, Calif., 1972), pp. 292–299.

13. Charles Tilly, *From Mobilization to Revolution* (Reading, Mass., 1978), p. 192.

originally religious concept of *yonaoshi*, or "world rectification."[14] There is evidence of peasants elsewhere in Japan evoking the presence of a "world rectification god" (*yonaoshi kami*) at least a half century before the Meiji Restoration. According to Sasaki Junnosuke, the earliest textual reference is found in an 1811 movement in Oka fief, Bingo province, while the first record of peasants using *yonaoshi* as a unifying force and source of authority is the uprising that took place in the Kamo region of Mikawa province in 1836. There are even earlier examples of the closely related "world leveling" (*yonarashi*) movements that date back to the mid-eighteenth century. But most of the movements belong to the period immediately preceding the overthrow of the Bakufu: those of 1866 in Chichibu and Shindatsu districts; of 1868 in Kozuke, Echigo, and Aizu regions; and of 1869 in Mino province and 1870 in the Shinshū region.[15]

Unlike benevolence, the concept of *yonaoshi* was not part of the ideology and symbology of seigneurial rule. The significance of the appearance of *yonaoshi* is twofold. First, precisely because the received ideology could not function effectively to protect them against sudden, market-induced crises, peasants reached beyond the established political culture to grasp religious symbols. Second, as Sasaki Junnosuke has observed, most of the movements occurred in the midst of a revolutionary situation.[16] Peasants could not act as a class; yet, sensing the historical bankruptcy of the Tokugawa polity and political economy, small peasants, according to Yasumaro Yoshio, "placed their hopes for the future in the world of the illusional community of *yonaoshi* which would universally save the people."[17]

It is significant that the potency of the idea of world rectification increased as the feudal polity declined. In the 1866 uprisings in Shindatsu and Chichibu districts there is very little doc-

14. Irwin Scheiner, "The Mindful Peasant," *Journal of Asian Studies* 32 (February 1973): 585–586.

15. Sasaki Junnosuke, "Bakumatsu no shakai jōsei to yonaoshi," *Iwanami kōza Nihon rekishi*, vol. 13 (1977): 305.

16. Sasaki, *Yonaoshi*, p. 108.

17. Yasumaro Yoshio, *Nihon no kindaika to minshū shisō* (Tokyo, 1974), p. 88.

umentary evidence that the peasants initially used the language of *yonaoshi* to articulate their purpose. In the case of the Shindatsu uprising, none of the primary sources mentions the term, and according to Sasaki the four references to *yonaoshi* in primary sources for the Chichibu uprising are textually suspect since they are found in the diaries of persons who were very likely not direct witnesses.[18] But there is no doubt that at a later date the peasants of Shindatsu referred to Kanno Hachirō, their leader, as a *daimyōjin*, "divine agent" and peasants in Chichibu and neighboring districts talked of the event as a *yonaoshi* uprising. It would appear that the greater the political space created by the collapse of Tokugawa authority, the more powerful the idea became.

Nevertheless, no matter how radical in conception, most *yonaoshi* uprisings did not lead to collective action beyond moral economy–type demands for sharing wealth and punishing the immoral rich, and "world rectification" ended when the crowd itself dispersed. Whatever the ideological break with the received tradition, there was no concomitant breakthrough to mobilization.

The *yonaoshi* movement in Aizu, however, was a notable exception, for there, as we have seen, the peasants created structures intended to bring about lasting changes. Instead of merely destroying the property of village headmen and moneylenders, they ousted the hereditary headmen and elected their peers, rescheduled old debts, regulated contracts between pawnbrokers and their clients, and either ordered the return of mortgaged land or modified the terms to protect the tenants.

Several factors appear to explain the unique direction of the movement in Aizu. First, the peasants in Aizu enjoyed extraordinary latitude for political mobilization. The defeat and expulsion of the daimyo Matsudaira Katamori and his entire corps of retainers eliminated all at once the feudal ruling class, and Meiji officials, busy reorganizing the central functions of administration, did not show any interest in intervening in village disputes. Second, social stratification in Aizu villages corre-

18. Sasaki, "Bakumatsu," p. 262.

sponded to patterns typical of early Tokugawa Japan, that is, before extensive development of peasant commodity production.[19] Tightly administered, heavily taxed, and distant from centers of trade, villages in Aizu were poorer than those in Shindatsu but also more homogeneous and integrated. Typically there was a large middle stratum of farm families whose holdings were of sufficient size to provide most of their subsistence needs; the upper and lower strata were correspondingly small. The greater part of the arable land was used to grow rice and other cereals, crops which required cooperative labor, in contrast to those specialty crops and by-employments whose production was concentrated entirely within individual households. Peasants in Aizu participated in the market, yet their survival depended on how local resources were managed, and not on the workings of national and international markets. We can speculate, therefore, that the social basis for reform aimed at restoring the vitality of the landed economy had not disintegrated under the pull of market relations. Unlike the highly stratified villages of Shindatsu where collective action was episodic and the intensity of mobilization was offset by lack of direction and short duration, Aizu peasants, once they had overthrown the traditional village leadership, could use the actual community to put into effect changes in political and economic relations which promised lasting relief. As we noted in chapter 7, the world of "world rectification" in Aizu was the village and not the state, but at least it was a real world and not an imaginary one of perfect benevolence.

Despite the ideological and strategic limits to collective action, peasant movements hastened the collapse of Tokugawa feudalism, at least indirectly. The majority of peasant uprisings in the critical period between 1866 and 1869 occurred in eastern Japan in areas administered by the Bakufu and fiefs of daimyo traditionally allied with the Tokugawa house.[20] The re-

19. Shōji Kichinosuke, *Meiji ishin no keizai kōzō* (Tokyo, 1954), p. 294.
20. Yoshio Sugimoto, "Structural Sources of Popular Revolts and the *Tōbaku* Movement at the Time of the Meiji Restoration," *Journal of Asian Studies* 34 (August 1975): 886–887.

gional pattern of these peasant uprisings is explained by the fact that the peasants were, by and large, in sericulture districts where they faced short-term credit and subsistence crises due to market forces. Nevertheless, widespread disorder in Tokugawa lands discredited the Bakufu, which had already lost legitimacy due to its failure to hold the imperialist powers at bay. Many daimyo feared that a prolonged civil war between pro-emperor and Bakufu forces would make it much more difficult to maintain law and order. The reluctance of most of the shogun's hereditary vassals to support the campaigns against Chōshū, the alacrity with which the expeditionary force sued for peace, and the almost universal acceptance of the Meiji regime all suggest that whether *fudai* or *tozama,* daimyo were influenced by the crescendo of localized rural revolts. Clearly a new government capable of uniting the country and reasserting central authority was needed, and not merely because of the foreign threat.

It can also be argued that the cumulative effects of several centuries of peasant protests created conditions favorable to radical change. Resistance by peasants to increased exploitation eventually limited the effectiveness of the *kokudaka* system of taxation. If samurai incomes did not fall in absolute terms, they declined drastically, compared with those of merchants and upper-status peasants. Institutionally and individually the samurai class became the clients of commoners who, not infrequently, made humiliating demands before agreeing to refinance old loans.[21] It is difficult to explain the radicalism of the young samurai who seized power in 1868—they dismantled the feudal polity within three years—without taking into account the impoverishment of the samurai class.

The rising number of peasant protests and the increased disorder of collective action in the late Tokugawa period signified not the intensification of class conflict—between the ruling class and the peasantry—but of conflict between strata of the peasant class as they competed for advantage in a complex mar-

21. For a most interesting example see Kozo Yamamura, *A Study of Samurai Income and Entrepreneurship* (Cambridge, Mass., 1974), pp. 47–48.

ket economy. In fact, in many areas stratification and differentiation of the rural population had reached the point where the category "peasant class," while still meaningful in the eyes of rulers, no longer designated a collectivity bound together by common interests and culture arising out of primary economic relationships.

In Japan in the 1860s the intensity of conflict among peasants had particular implications for political change. The Meiji Restoration differed from the great revolutions of the modern era—France, Russia, China—in that the destruction of feudalism and subsequent modernization was not accompanied by social revolution, but by a shift of power within elite political classes. Peasant revolts in France, Russia, and China, according to Theda Skocpol, "destroyed the old agrarian class relations and undermined the political and military supports for liberalism and counterrevolution. They opened the way for marginal political elites, perhaps supported by urban popular movements, to consolidate the Revolutions on the basis of centralized and mass-incorporating state organizations."[22] But peasant uprisings in Japan did not have the power to destroy dominant class relations, for poor peasants attacked wealthy peasants whose power was entirely local. Though widespread and individually ferocious, the uprisings did not shake the social foundations of the ancient regime. The aim of small peasants was the preservation of their present status as small proprietors; if anything, they assumed the seigneurial class to be sympathetic to their needs. Thus, despite extensive destruction of property, the revolts by small peasant farmers did not create conditions which favored the emergence of socially and politically marginal groups who, if able to seize power, might have carried out a social revolution.

22. Theda Skocpol, *States and Social Revolutions* (Cambridge, 1979), p. 112.

Bibliography

Collected Documents

Aizu nōmin ikki: Shiryō shūsei [Peasant movements in Aizu: Collected documents], vols. 1–2. Edited by Tashiro Shigeo. Aizu-Wakamatsu: Rekishi Shunjūsha, 1978.

Aizu-Wakamatsu shi [Aizu-Wakamatsu history], vol. 8, *Shiryō 1* [Documents 1]. Edited by Toyoda Takeshi. Aizu-Wakamatsu: Aizu-Wakamatsu Shi Shuppan Iinkai, 1967.

Fukushima-ken shi [Fukushima prefecture history], vol. 9, *Kinsei shiryō 2* [Early modern documents 2]. Fukushima: Fukushima Prefecture, 1965. Idem, vol. 10, pt. 2, *Kinsei shiryō 4*, 1968.

Fukushima-shi shi [Fukushima city history], vol. 7, *Kinsei shiryō 1* [Early modern documents 1]. Fukushima: Fukushima-shi Kyōiku Iinkai, 1970. Idem, vol. 8, *Kinsei shiryō 2*, 1968. Idem, vol. 9, *Kinsei shiryō 3*, 1971.

Minshū undō no shisō [The thought of popular movements]. Edited by Shōji Kichinosuke, Hayashi Motoi, and Yasumaro Yoshio. Tokyo: Iwanami Shoten, 1970.

Nihon shomin seikatsu shiryō shūsei [Collected documents on commoner life in Japan], vol. 6, *Ikki* [Collective action]. Edited by Aoki Kōji et al. Tokyo: San'ichi Shobō, 1968.

Tōhoku shohan hyakushō ikki kenkyū: Shiryō shūsei [Research on peasant movements in fiefs of northeastern Japan: Collected documents]. Edited by Shōji Kichinosuke. Tokyo: Ochanomizu Shobō, 1969.

Local Histories

Aizu-Wakamatsu shi [History of Aizu-Wakamatsu], vol. 2, *Kizukareta Aizu han* [The building of Aizu fief]. Edited by Toyoda Takeshi. Aizu-Wakamatsu: Aizu-Wakamatsu Shi Shuppan Iinkai, 1965. Idem, vol. 3, *Aizu han no kakuritsu* [The consolidation of Aizu fief], 1965. Idem, vol. 4, *Aizu hansei no tenkai* [Changes in Aizu fief rule], 1966. Idem, vol. 5, *Gekidō suru Aizu* [Aizu in turmoil], 1966.

Fukushima-ken shi [Fukushima prefecture history], vol. 2, *Kinsei 1* [Early modern 1]. Fukushima: Fukushima Prefecture, 1971. Idem, vol. 3, *Kinsei 2*, 1970. Idem, vol. 22, *Jinbutsu* [Famous people], 1972.

Fukushima-shi shi [Fukushima city history], vol. 2, *Kinsei 1* [Early modern 1]. Fukushima: Fukushima-shi Kyōiku Iinkai, 1972. Idem, vol. 3, *Kinsei 2*, 1973.

Yokohama-shi shi [Yokohama city history], vol. 2. Edited by Oikawa Morio. Yokohama: Yurindo, 1959.

Books and Articles in Japanese

Abe Makoto and Sakai Hajime. "Hōkensei no dōyō" [The shaking of the feudal system]. In *Iwanami kōza Nihon rekishi*, vol. 12, pp. 1–51. Tokyo: Iwanami Shoten, 1976.

Andō Seiichi. *Edo jidai no nōmin* [Peasants of the Edo period]. Tokyo: Yoshikawa Kōbunkan, 1966.

Aoki Kōji. *Hyakushō ikki no nenjiteki kenkyū* [Chronological study of peasant movements]. Tokyo: Shinseisha, 1966.

———. *Hyakushō ikki sōgō nenpyō* [Comprehensive chronology of peasant movements]. Tokyo: San'ichi Shobō, 1971.

Aoki Michio. "Bakumatsu ni okeru nōmin tōsō to nōheisei" [The peasant militia system and peasant struggles in the Bakumatsu period]. In *Ronshū Nihonshi*, vol. 8, *Bakuhan taisei*, ed. Odachi Uki, pp. 305–323. Tokyo: Yūseido, 1973.

———. "Keiō ninen Ushū Murayama chihō no yonaoshi ikki" [The *yonaoshi* movement in Ushū Murayama in 1866]. In *Murakata sōdō to yonaoshi*, vol. 1, edited by Sasaki Junnosuke, pp. 162–209. Tokyo: Aoki Shoten, 1972.

Araki Moriaki. *Bakuhan taisei shakai no seiritsu to kōzō* [The establishment and structure of the Tokugawa polity]. Tokyo: Ochanomizu Shobō, 1959.

———. "Yōsangyō no tenkai to Tokugawa ki no jinushisei kosaku kankei" [The change in sericulture and Tokugawa landlord-tenant relations]. In *Yōsangyō no hattatsu to kisei jinushisei*, edited by Furushima Toshio and Takahashi Kōhachirō, pp. 111–185. Tokyo: Ochanomizu Shobō, 1958.

Arizumi Sadao. "Yōsan chitai no nōgyō kōzō" [The structure of agriculture in sericulture districts]. In *Bakumatsu ishin no nōgyō kōzō*, edited by Horie Hideichi, pp. 191–252. Tokyo: Iwanami Shoten, 1963.

Doi Hiroshi. "Bakuhansei kaitaiki ni okeru murakata sōdō no rekishiteki igi" [The historical significance of villagers' struggles during the dissolution of the Tokugawa polity]. In *Rekishigaku kenkyū*, special volume, "Rekishi ninshiki ni okeru jinmin tōsō no shiten," November 1972, pp. 118–124.

Fujita Jōji. "Bakuhansei ryōshu ron" [Debate on lordship in the Tokugawa polity]. *Nihonshi kenkyū* 139 (March 1974): 158–175.

Fukaya Katsumi. "Bakuhansei ni okeru muraukesei no tokushitsu to nōmin tōsō" [Peasant struggles and the special features of the system of village tax assessment]. *Rekishigaku kenkyū: Bessatsu tokushū* (November 1972): 99–117.

———. "Bakuhansei shakai no kaikyu tōsōshi kenkyū ni tsuite" [Concerning research on the history of class struggle of the Tokugawa polity]. *Rekishi hyōron* 289 (May 1974): 22–35.

———. "Hyakushō ikki" [Peasant movements]. In *Iwanami kōza Nihon rekishi*, vol. 11, pp. 102–137. Tokyo: Iwanami Shoten, 1976.

———. *Hyakushō ikki no rekishiteki kōzō* [Historical structure of peasant movements]. Tokyo: Azekura Shobō, 1979.

Fukaya, Kiyoshi. *Kinsei Nihon no minshū rinri shisō* [Ethical popular thought of the early modern period]. Tokyo: Kōbundō, 1973.

Furushima Toshio. "Bakufu zaisei shūnyū no dōkō to nōmin shūdatsu" [Shifts in Bakufu financial revenue and exploitation of the peasantry]. In *Nihon keizaishi taikei*, vol. 4, edited by Furushima Toshio, pp. 3–44. Tokyo: Tokyo Daigaku Shuppankai, 1965.

———. "Kinsei keizaishi sōron" [General discussion of early modern economic history]. In *Nihon keizaishi taikei*, vol. 3, edited by Furushima Toshio, pp. 1–56. Tokyo: Tokyo Daigaku Shuppankai, 1965.

———. *Nihon jinushisei shi kenkyū* [Research on the history of Japan's landlord system]. Tokyo: Iwanami Shoten, 1958.

———. *Nihon nōgyō gijutsu shi* [History of Japanese agricultural technology], vol. 2. Tokyo: Jichōsha, 1949.

————. "Shōhin ryūtsu no hatten to ryōshu keizai" [Development of the circulation of commodities and seigneurial finances]. In *Iwanami kōza Nihon rekishi*, vol. 12, kinsei 4, pp. 53–102. Tokyo: Iwanami Shoten, 1963.

Hara Shōgo. "Bakuhansei kokka no seiritsu ni tsuite" [The formation of the nation in the Tokugawa polity]. In *Ronshū Nihon rekishi*, vol. 7, *Bakuhan taisei 1*, edited by Odachi Uki, pp. 41–61. Tokyo: Yūseido, 1973.

Hayama Teisaku. "Kinsei zenki no nōgyō seisan to nōmin seikatsu" [Agricultural production and peasant life in the early half of the early modern period]. In *Iwanami kōza Nihon rekishi*, vol. 10, pp. 173–211. Tokyo: Iwanami Shoten, 1975.

Hayashi Motoi. "Hōreki-Tenmei no shakai jōsei" [Social conditions of the Hōreki-Tenmei period]. In *Iwanami kōza Nihon rekishi*, vol. 12, pp. 103–154. Tokyo: Iwanami Shoten, 1963.

Hiromatsu Yoshiro. "Kinsei hō" [Early modern law]. In *Iwanami kōza Nihon rekishi*, vol. 11, pp. 332–338. Tokyo: Iwanami Shoten, 1976.

Hirasawa Kyoto. *Kinsei sonraku e no ikō to heinō bunri* [Separation of warrior and farmer and the transition to the early modern village]. Tokyo: Azekura Shobō, 1973.

Horie Hideichi. *Bakumatsu ishin no nōgyō kōzō* [Agricultural structure of the Bakumatsu period and the Restoration]. Tokyo: Iwanami Shoten, 1963.

Itō Tadashi. "Kenchi to nōmin shihai" [Land surveys and rule of the peasantry]. In *Nihon keizaishi taikei*, vol. 3, edited by Furushima Toshio, pp. 171–218. Tokyo: Tokyo Daigaku Shuppankai, 1965.

Itō Tasaburō. "Kinsei daimyō kenkyū josetsu" [Introduction to research on early modern daimyo], pts. 1 and 2. *Shigaku zasshi* 55 (September 1944): 899–944, and 57 (November 1944): 1170–1230.

Kanō Tanboku [Uegaki Morikuni]. *Yōsan hiroku* [Confidential record of silkworm rearing]. See Ouekaki in English and French section.

Kidota Shirō. "Kōshin chitai ni okeru burujoateki hatten to gōnōsō" [Bourgeois-like development in backward areas and the wealthy-peasant stratum]. *Nihonshi kenkyū* 151 (March 1975): 166–183.

Kimura Motoi. "Chōsan to utae" [Mass flights and appeals]. In *Iwanami kōza Nihon rekishi*, vol. 10, pp. 214–244. Tokyo: Iwanami Shoten, 1975.

Kitajima Masamoto. *Edo Bakufu no kenryoku kōzō* [The authority structure of the Edo Bakufu]. Tokyo: Iwanami Shoten, 1959.

_____. "Heinō bunri to bakuhan taisei" [Separation of warrior and farmer and the *bakuhan* system]. In *Ronshū Nihon rekishi*, vol. 7, pp. 19–29. Tokyo: Yūseido, 1973.

Kobayashi Seiji. "Bakuhan taisei seiritsu no sobyō" [Sketch of the establishment of the *bakuhan* system]. In *Ronshū Nihon rekishi*, vol. 7, pp. 30–40. Tokyo: Yūseido, 1973.

Kodama Kōta. "Mibun to kazoku" [Status and family]. In *Iwanami kōza Nihon rekishi*, vol. 10, pp. 223–271. Tokyo: Iwanami Shoten, 1963.

_____. *Kinsei nōmin seikatsu shi* [History of early modern peasant life]. Tokyo: Yoshikawa Kōbunkan, 1957.

Minegishi Sumio. "Ikkō ikki" [Ikkō uprisings]. In *Iwanami kōza Nihon rekishi*, vol. 8, pp. 127–171. Tokyo: Iwanami Shoten, 1976.

Mizumoto Kunihoko. "Shoki murakata sōdō to kinsei sonraku" [Intravillage struggles of the early Tokugawa period]. *Nihonshi kenkyū* 139–140 (March 1974): 175–193.

Morita Takeshi. "Bakumatsu-Meiji shonen no nōmin tōsō— Fukushima Shindatsu chihō ni tsuite" [Peasant struggles in Bakumatsu and early Meiji—With reference to the Shindatsu district of Fukushima]. In *Murakata sōdō to yonaoshi*, vol. 1, edited by Sasaki Junnosuke, pp. 211–246. Tokyo: Aoki Shoten, 1972.

_____. "Chokkatsu ken ni okeru Meiji seifu no keizai seisaku" [The economic policy of the Meiji government in prefectures under direct rule]. *Rekishigaku kenkyū* 359 (April 1970): 16–27.

Muroi Yasuhiro. "Minamiyama okurairi sōdō oboegaki" [Memorandum on the okurairi disturbance in Minamiyama]. *Fukushima shigaku kenkyū fukkan* 9 (November 1969): 27–32.

Ōguchi Yūjirō. "Bakumatsu ni okeru yōsangyō no hattatsu to nōson kōzō" [The development of sericulture and village structure in the Bakumatsu period]. *Tochi seidō shigaku* 19 (April 1963): 38–54.

Ōishi Kaichirō. "Meiji zenki ni okeru sanshugyō no hatten to kisei jinushisei" [The silkworm-egg-card industry in early Meiji and the development of the parasitic landlord system]. In *Yōsangyō no hattatsu to kisei jinushisei*, edited by Furushima Toshio and Takahashi Kōhachirō, pp. 327–423. Tokyo: Ochanomizu Shobō, 1958.

_____. *Nihon chihō zaigyōsei shi josetsu* [Introduction to the political economy of rural Japan]. Tokyo: Ochanomizu Shobō, 1961.

Ōishi Shinzaburō. *Kinsei sonraku no kōzō to kaseido* [The structure of the early modern village and the family system]. Tokyo: Ochanomizu Shobō, 1968.

————. *Kyōhō kaikaku no keizai seisaku* [The economic policy of the Kyōhō reform]. Tokyo: Ochanomizu Shobō, 1961.

————. "Yōsan shijō ni tsuite" [Concerning the sericulture market]. In *Yōsangyō no hattatsu to kisei jinushisei,* edited by Furushima Toshio and Takahashi Kōhachirō, pp. 297–326. Tokyo: Ochanomizu Shobō, 1958.

Ōishi Yūjirō. "Shōhin seisan no hatten to nōson no henshitsu" [The development of commodity production and qualitative changes in the village]. In *Nihon keizai taikei,* vol. 4, edited by Furushima Toshio, pp. 263–300. Tokyo: Ochanomizu Shobō, 1965.

Sasaki Hajime. "Kōshin chitai no nōgyō kōzō: Aizu o chūshin toshite" [The agriculture structure of backward areas, with a focus on Aizu]. In *Bakumatsu Ishin no nōgyō kōzō,* edited by Horie Hideichi, pp. 252–300. Tokyo: Iwanami Shoten, 1963.

Sasaki Junnosuke. *Bakuhan kenryoku no kiso kōzō* [The fundamental structure of political authority in the Tokugawa polity]. Tokyo: Aoki Shoten, 1964.

————. "Bakuhan taisei no kōzōteki tokushitsu" [The structural characteristics of the *bakuhan* system]. In *Ronshū Nihon rekishi,* vol. 7, *Bakuhan taisei I,* edited by Odachi Uki, pp. 1–15. Tokyo: Yūseido, 1973.

————. "Bakumatsu no shakai jōsei to yonaoshi" [The social conditions of Bakumatsu society and world rectification]. In *Iwanami kōza Nihon rekishi,* vol. 13, pp. 247–299. Tokyo: Iwanami Shoten, 1977.

————. "Hōreki-Kansei ki ni okeru sanshu keiei" [Management of silkworm-egg card (production) in the Hōreki-Kansei period]. In *Yōsangyō no hattatsu to kisei jinushisei,* edited by Furushima Toshio and Takahashi Kōhachirō, pp. 229–296. Tokyo: Ochanomizu Shobō, 1958.

————. "Kinsei nōson no seiritsu" [The formation of the early modern village]. In *Iwanami kōza Nihon rekishi,* vol. 10, pp. 165–221. Tokyo: Iwanami Shoten, 1963.

————. "Seiritsu ki bakuhansei no chiiki kubun to nōminteki sho yōkyū" [Regional differences and demands of peasants during the founding period of the Tokugawa polity]. In *Nihon Keizai shi,* vol. 3, ed. Furushima Toshio, pp. 253–300. Tokyo: Tokyo Daigaku Shuppankai, 1965.

————. *Yonaoshi* [World rectification]. Tokyo: Iwanami Shoten, 1979.

————. "Yonaosho no jōkyō" [The conditions of *yonaoshi*]. In *Kōza Nihon shi,* vol. 5, edited by Nihonshi Kenkyūkai, pp. 87–112. Tokyo:

Tokyo Daigaku Shuppankai, 1970.

———, ed. *Murakata sōdō to yonaoshi* [Villagers' struggles and world rectification], vol. 1. Tokyo: Aoki Shoten, 1972.

Shōji Kichinosuke. "Aizu han ni okeru tochi bunkyūsei" [The land-distribution system in Aizu fief]. *Rekishigaku kenkyū* 103 (September 1953): 19–53.

———. "Hōken shakai ni okeru kōgyō no seisan keitai" [The form of industry production in feudal society]. *Shōgaku ronshū* 23 (May 1954): 50–85.

———. *Kinsei minshū shisō no kenkyū* [Research on early modern popular thought]. Tokyo: Azekura Shobō, 1979.

———. *Kinsei yōsangyō hattatsu shi* [History of the development of the early modern sericulture industry]. Tokyo: Ochanomizu Shobō, 1964.

———. *Meiji Ishin no keizai kōzō* [The economic structure of the Meiji Restoration]. Tokyo: Ochanomizu Shobō, 1954.

———. "Shōhin seisan no hatten to kisei jinushisei no seiritsu" [The development of commodity production and the establishment of the parasitic landlord system]. *Shōgaku ronshū* 23, no. 5 (1955): 145–231.

———. *Yonaoshi ikki no kenkyū* [Research on *yonaoshi* movements]. Tokyo: Azekura Shobō, 1970.

Takagi Shōsaku. "Bakuhan taisei daiichi dankai kara daini dankai e no suikō ni tsuite" [Concerning the transition from the first to the second stage of the *bakuhan* system]. In *Ronshū Nihon rekishi*, vol. 7, pp. 194–217. Tokyo: Yūseido, 1973.

Yamada Shun. *Nihon hōkensei no kōzō bunseki* [Structural analysis of Japan's feudal system]. Tokyo: Miraisha, 1956.

———. "Sanshu seisan ni okeru han-hōkenteki keiei" [Semifeudal management in silkworm-egg-card production]. In *Yōsangyō no hattatsu to kinsei jinushisei*, edited by Furushima Toshio and Takahashi Kōhachirō, pp. 187–228. Tokyo: Ochanomizu Shobō, 1958.

———. "Shindatsu chihō no sanshugyō" [The silkworm-egg-card industry in Shindatsu]. In *Nihon sangyō shi taikei*, vol. 5, pp. 73–94. Tokyo: Tokyo Daigaku Shuppankai, 1960.

Yamaguchi Kōhei. "Aizu Minamiyama okurairi nōmin sōdō no shuin taru kaimai ni tsuite no kenkyū" [Research concerning the causal role of *kaimai* in peasant disturbances in the Aizu Minamiyama district]. *Aizu shi dankai* 31 (September 1956): 12–54.

Yamazaki Ryūzō. "Edo kōki ni okeru nōson keizai no hatten to nōminsō no bunkai" [The development of the village economy in the later Edo period and the disintegration of the peasant class]. In *Iwanami kōza Nihon rekishi,* vol. 12, pp. 331–374. Tokyo: Iwanami Shoten, 1963.

Yasumaro Yoshio. "Minshū hōki no sekai zō" [The world-view of popular uprisings]. *Shisō,* April 1973, pp. 94–119.

————. *Nihon no kindaika to minshū shisō* [Japan's modernization and popular thought]. Tokyo: Aoki Shoten, 1974.

Yoshida Isamu, *Satō Tomonobu* [Satō Tomonobu]. Aizu-Wakamatsu: Rekishi Shunju Sha, 1979.

Books and Articles in English and French

Alavi, Hamza. "Peasant Classes and Primordial Loyalties." *Journal of Peasant Studies* 1 (October 1973): 23–62.

Anderson, Perry. *Lineages of the Absolutist State.* London: New Left Review, 1974.

Black, Edwin. "The Second Persona." *Quarterly Journal of Speech* 2 (April 1970): 109–119.

Borton, Hugh. *Peasant Uprisings in Japan of the Tokugawa Period.* Originally published in *Transactions of the Asiatic Society of Japan,* vol. 16, Tokyo, 1938. Reprint., New York: Paragon Book Reprint Corp., 1968.

Boxer, C. R. *The Christian Century in Japan, 1549–1650.* Berkeley and Los Angeles: University of California Press, 1974.

Brinton, Crane. *The Anatomy of Revolution.* New York: Norton, 1938.

Burton, W. Donald. "Peasant Movements in Early Tokugawa Japan." *Journal of Peasant Studies* 8, no. 3 (1979): 162–181.

Chayanov, A. V. *The Theory of Peasant Economy.* Edited by Basile Kerblay, R. E. F. Smith, and Daniel Thorner. American Economic Association, Homewood, Ill.: R. D. Irwin, 1966.

Frost, Peter. *The Bakumatsu Currency Crisis.* Cambridge, Mass.: Harvard University Press, 1970.

Gotsch, Carl H. "Technical Change and the Distribution of Income in Rural Areas." *American Journal of Agriculture Economics* 54 (May 1972): 326–341.

Greenough, Paul. *Prosperity and Misery in Modern India: Bengal Famine of 1943–44.* New York: Oxford University Press, 1981.

Griffin, Keith. *Political Economy of Agrarian Change.* Cambridge, Mass.: Harvard University Press, 1974.

Gurr, Ted Robert. *Why Men Rebel.* Princeton, N.J.: Princeton University Press, 1970.

Hall, John W., Nagahara Kenji, and Yamamura Kozo, eds. *Japan before Tokugawa*. Princeton, N.J.: Princeton University Press, 1981.

Hall, John W., and Jansen, Marius B., eds. *Studies in the Institutional History of Early Modern Japan*. Princeton, N.J.: Princeton University Press, 1968.

Hanley, Susan, and Yamamura, Kozo. *Economic and Demographic Change in Premodern Japan 1600–1868*. Princeton, N.J.: Princeton University Press, 1977.

Harrison, Mark. "The Peasant Mode of Production in the Work of A. V. Chayanov." *Journal of Peasant Studies* 4 (July 1977): 323–336.

Hashimoto, Mitsuru. "The Social Background of Peasant Uprisings in Tokugawa Japan." In *Conflict in Modern Japanese History*, edited by Tetsuo Najita and J. Victor Koschmann, pp. 145–163. Princeton, N.J.: Princeton University Press, 1982.

Hinton, Rodney H. "Peasant Society, Peasant Movements and Feudalism in Medieval Europe." In *Rural Protest*, edited by Henry Landsberger, pp. 67–94. London: Macmillan, 1974.

Hobsbawm, Eric J. "Peasants and Politics." *Journal of Peasant Studies* 1 (October 1973): 3–22.

Johnson, Chalmers. *Revolutionary Change*. Boston: Little, Brown, 1966.

Kanō Tanboku [Uegaki Morikuni]. See Ouekaki, below.

Kaplan, Temma. *Anarchists of Andalusia*. Princeton, N.J.: Princeton University Press, 1977.

Landsberger, Henry. "Peasant Unrest: Themes and Variations." In *Rural Protest: Peasant Movements and Social Change*, ed. H. Landsberger, pp. 1–64. London: Macmillan, 1974.

Lupsha, Peter. "Explanations of Political Violence: Some Psychological Theories versus Indignation." *Politics and Society* 2 (1971): 89–104.

Oberschall, Anthony. *Social Conflict and Social Movements*. Englewood Cliffs, N.J.: Prentice-Hall, 1973.

Ouekaki Morikouni [Uegaki Morikuni, pen name of Kanō Tanboku]. *Yo-san-fi-rok*. Translated by Johann Joseph Hoffmann. Paris: Bouchard-Huzard, 1848.

Paige, Jeffrey M. *Agrarian Revolution: Social Movements and Export Agriculture in the Underdeveloped World*. New York: Free Press, 1975.

Popkin, Samuel L. *The Rational Peasant: The Political Economy of Rural Society in Vietnam*. Berkeley and Los Angeles: University of California Press, 1979.

Scheiner, Irwin. "Benevolent Lords and Honorable Peasants: Rebellion and Peasant Consciousness in Tokugawa Japan." In *Japanese*

Thought in the Tokugawa Period, 1600–1868, edited by Tetsuo Najita and Irwin Scheiner, pp. 39–62. Chicago: University of Chicago Press, 1978.

———. "The Mindful Peasant: Sketches for a Study of Rebellion." *Journal of Asian Studies* 32 (August 1973): 579–591.

Scott, James C. "The Erosion of Patron-Client Bonds and Social Change in Rural Southeast Asia." *Journal of Asian Studies* 32 (November 1972): 5–37.

———. *The Moral Economy of the Peasant: Rebellion and Subsistence in Southeast Asia.* New Haven, Conn.: Yale University Press, 1976.

Sipple, Patricia. "Popular Protest in Early Modern Japan: The Bushū Outburst." *Harvard Journal of Asian Studies* 37 (December 1978): 273–322.

Skocpol, Theda. *States and Social Revolutions: A Comparative Analysis of France, Russia and China.* Cambridge: Cambridge University Press, 1979.

Smith, Thomas C. *The Agrarian Origins of Modern Japan.* Stanford, Calif.: Stanford University Press, 1979.

———. "Farm Family By-Employments." *Journal of Economic History* 29 (December 1969): 687–715.

———. "The Land Tax in the Tokugawa Period." In *Studies in the Institutional History of Early Modern Japan,* edited by John W. Hall and Marius B. Jansen, pp. 283–299. Princeton, N.J.: Princeton University Press, 1968.

———. *Nakahara.* Stanford, Calif.: Stanford University Press, 1977.

———. "Ōkura Nagatsune and the Technologists." In *Personalities in Japanese History,* edited by Albert Craig and Donald Shively, pp. 127–154. Berkeley and Los Angeles: University of California Press, 1970.

Stavenhagen, Rudolfo. *Social Classes in Agrarian Societies.* Garden City, N.Y.: Anchor Books, 1975.

Stinchcombe, Arthur L. "Agricultural Enterprise and Rural Class Relations." *American Journal of Sociology* 62 (September 1961): 165–176.

Sugimoto, Yoshio. "Structural Sources of Popular Revolts and the Tōbaku Movement at the Time of the Meiji Restoration." *Journal of Asian Studies* 34 (August 1975): 875–889.

Tanaka, Yoshimaro. *Sericology.* Bombay: Central Silk Board, 1964.

Thompson, E. P. "The Moral Economy of the English Crowd in the Eighteenth Century." *Past and Present* 50 (February 1971): 71–133.

Tilly, Charles. *From Mobilization to Revolution*. Reading, Mass.: Addison-Wesley, 1978.

———. Tilly, Louise, and Tilly, Richard. *The Rebellious Century.* Cambridge, Mass.: Harvard University Press, 1975.

Walthall, Anne. "Times of Protest: Commoners and Collective Action in Late Eighteenth Century Japan." Ph.D. diss., University of Chicago, 1978.

Wolf, Eric R. "Closed Corporate Peasant Communities in Mesoamerica and Central Java." *Southwestern Journal of Anthropology* 13 (1957): 1–18.

———. *Peasants*. Englewood Cliffs, N.J.: Prentice-Hall, 1966.

Yamamura, Kozo. *A Study of Samurai Income and Entrepreneurship.* Cambridge, Mass.: Harvard University Press, 1974.

Zolberger, Aristide R. "Movements of Madness." *Politics and Society* 2 (1972): 183–297.

Index